Son Of God

George Natar

Son Of God

By Divine Hereditary Methodology

George Natar

Adelaide
2022

Text copyright © 2022 remains with the author, George Natar, and for the collection with ATF Theology. All rights reserved. Except for any fair dealing permitted under the Copyright Act, no part of the publication may be reproduced by any means without prior permission. Inquiries should be made in the first instance with the publisher.

A Forum for Theology in the World
Volume 9, Issue 1, 2022

A Forum for Theology in the World is an academic refereed journal aimed at engaging with issues in the contemporary world, a world which is pluralist and ecumenical in nature. The journal reflects this pluralism and ecumenism. Each edition is theme specific and has its own editor responsible for the production. The journal aims to elicit and encourage dialogue on topics and issues in contemporary society and within a variety of religious traditions. The Editor in Chief welcomes submissions of manuscripts, collections of articles, for review from individuals or institutions, which may be from seminars or conferences or written specifically for the journal. An internal peer review is expected before submitting the manuscript. It is the expectation of the publisher that, once a manuscript has been accepted for publication, it will be submitted according to the house style to be found at the back of this volume. All submissions to the Editor in Chief are to be sent to: hdregan@atf. org.au.

Each edition is available as a journal subscription, or as a book in print, pdf or epub, through the ATF Press web site — www.atfpress.com. Journal subscriptions are also available through EBSCO and other library suppliers.

Editor in Chief
Hilary Regan, ATF Press

A Forum for Theology in the World is published by ATF Theology and imprint of ATF (Australia) Ltd (ABN 90 116 359 963) and
is published twice or three times a year.

ISBN:	978-1-922737-37-3 soft
	978-1-922737-38-0 hard
	978-1-922737-39-7 epub
	978-1-922737-40-3 pdf

Published and edited by

THEOLOGY

Making a lasting impact

An imprint of the ATF Press Publishing Group
owned by ATF (Australia) Ltd.
PO Box 234
Brompton, SA 5007
Australia
ABN 90 116 359 963
www.atfpress.com

A Forum for Theology in the World Vol 9 No 1/2022

Table of Contents

Abbreviations	vii
Preface	ix
1. Introduction	1
2. Evidence for the Humanity of Jesus	11
The Natural Method of Jesus' Dying	12
Philological Evidence for Citing the Speared Side	16
The Meaning of the Flow of Blood and Water from Jesus' Side	20
3. Evidence for the Divinity of Jesus	29
Merciful Miracle Worker	29
Jesus the Son of man	30
Authoritative Statements	32
Jesus Worshipped	32
Paul's Perception of Jesus and God	35
Jesus' Resurrection	35
Jesus called 'God'	36
Jesus and the Jews	37
Jesus and Thomas	38
Emmanuel	39
'Your Throne, O God'	40
God Incarnate	41
The Only-Begotten God	41
4. A Methodology by Which Jesus Could Be Human and Divine	43
Humans and their DNA	43
Jesus' Possible Ontologies	45

A Humanistic Ontology	46
Adoptionism	48
A Specially Created Sperm	51
Incarnation	52
A Genetic Hereditary Methodology for the Divinity and Humanity of Jesus	63

5. God's Literal Fatherhood of Jesus — 69
    Logical Inference from Genetics and God's Motive for Atonement — 69
    The Testimony of Mary and Joseph — 70
    Jesus' Self-Consciousness of God as His Literal Father — 76

6. Objections to the Hypothesis of Divinity by a Genetic Methodology: The Pre-existence of Jesus — 83
    The Gospel of John — 84
    The Prologue of John — 87
    Philippians 2:6–11 — 96
    The Agency of Creation — 98
        I Corinthians 8:6 — 99
        Colossians 1:16–17 — 102
        Hebrews 1:2 — 103
        Hebrews 1:3 — 103

7. Implication for the Doctrine of the Trinity — 107

Conclusion — 119

Abbreviations

BCE Before the Christian (or Common) Era
CE Christian (or Common) Era
DJG Dictionary of Jesus and the Gospels
LCL Loeb Classical Library
LXX Septuagint
NIV New International Version (1978)
NRSV New Revised Standard Version (1989)
NT New Testament
OT Old Testament
PG Patrologia Graeca by JP Mige
TLG Thesaurus Linguae Graecae
WBC World Biblical Commentary

A Forum for Theology in the World Vol 9 No 1/2022

Preface

Humans are naturally curious about how things happen. This curiosity is fostered by some kind of scientific study. It is natural for a reader of the Bible to wonder how it was that a child was born from a human mother without a human father. The idea of parthenogenesis has been superseded as it does not occur in humans and the idea of cloning seems to have taken its place. But the offspring from such an event should be female, the same as the mother.

The Bible designates Jesus as the son of God and so, the most natural and logical deduction is that God contributed to Mary's child in some way. But metaphorical sonships of God have been expressed for centuries. However, the alternative possibility to this would consider that a contribution from God could have taken place by means of a hereditary and genetic method. This would make Jesus the literal child of God. The idea is important enough to be investigated with the provision of evidence. The result of that investigation is the writing of this book.

The intended reader is one who is inquisitive enough to want to understand the doctrine about the nature of Jesus that is put forward by churches in teaching and in song. Ideas that seem to be contradictory are often called mysteries. This implies that evidence for them is not required. Worse than this, it is thought that such things have already been settled in history and need no further investigation. But human curiosity searches for understanding.

It would be helpful if the reader of this book was also a Bible reader and may have some theological knowledge to understand biblical and theological terms used. It may be also useful, but not essential, for the reader to have some biological knowledge in order to understand some of the scientific explanations contained in some chapters.

The book may be classified as an apologetic work, an explanation for the support and the clarification of a doctrine. It seeks to answer the puzzle of why Jesus is sometimes called Son of God and son of man, and truly human and truly divine. Is it simply a title or is there some way by which he could have been literally human and divine? If Jesus is truly divine, how can we then believe in monotheism and say that there is only one God? These are questions that have exercised the minds of Christians since the early centuries of the church and some answers given have been contradictory to one another.

It is acknowledged that many worthwhile volumes have been written on this subject outlining the history of theological thought and debates that have taken place over time about the nature of Jesus. The present writing proposes a methodology by which the unique ontology of Jesus may have been achieved and the method by which this most significant emissary from God arrived in the world.

As a prologue to the methodology proposed, evidence for the humanity and for the divinity of Jesus is outlined. A hereditary methodology is then suggested and alternative methods are rejected because they lack evidence. Support for this methodology consists of biblical indications for Jesus' literal sonship from God and objections to the method are shown to arise from misinterpretations of some biblical texts. If the methodology is correct, the way a trinity of divine persons may be perceived is suggested.

Chapter One
Introduction

The investigation which has led to the writing of this book has sought to find clarity and reality in a narrow area of theology regarding Jesus of Nazareth. It confines itself to considerations surrounding his origin, the method of his coming and his nature rather than detailing aspects of his redemptive involvement. Nevertheless, it concludes that Jesus is a uniquely adequate and worthy redeemer of humankind. The epistemic considerations that follow are intended to give an idea of the kind of detail to be pursued in the rest of the book.

First, evidence for any proposition is indispensable for attaining knowledge of all kinds, be it scientific, historical or religious understanding. The constituents of knowledge are well known, but they are listed here as background to what follows. Belief forms the basis for all thought, religious and secular. A familiar saying that a proposition is accepted 'by faith' implies that it is believed without evidence. This is a misleading assumption because belief is part of all knowledge. A definition of knowing is that 'knowledge is justified true belief'.[1] Believing has been described as 'the resting of the mind on the sufficiency of the evidence'.[2] Therefore, belief justified by evidence, provides confidence for the reality of that which is believed.

The sufficiency of evidence may be debatable for the belief of many propositions such as the possibility of theism as well as various religious convictions resulting in Christianity, Judaism, Islam,

---

1. Anthony C Grayling, 'Epistemology' in *The Blackwell Companion to Philosophy*, second edition, edited by Nicholas Bunnin and EP Tsui-James (Oxford: Blackwell Publishing Company, 2003), 37–60.
2. Rudolph Nelson, *The Making and Unmaking of an Evangelical Mind: The Case of Edward Carnell* (Cambridge: Cambridge University Press, 1988), 140.

Buddhism, Hinduism and others. Their beliefs for achieving favour with a deity or for everlasting wellbeing do not coincide. Yet adherents may exercise an honest, if subjective, profound sense of trust in a holy object or person, an experience sometimes known as 'the numinous', even without adequate evidence. Although the experience of wonder and worship is real for a believer, in some situations the evidence for belief is insufficient to be convincing to logical thought.

The adjudicator for the sufficiency of evidence is the 'probability' for the truth of a proposal. It is calculated in order to put the mind at rest regarding the evidence before it. Probability for the sufficiency of evidence is an essential part of any scientific investigation. The practice of science demands a calculation of probability of ninety-five per cent or more for the belief of any proposition, while a hundred per cent amounts to certainty.

Evidence for repeatable events generates more confidence for the truth of belief than evidence for non-repeatable events. The explanatory power of the former depends on scientific experiments which can be repeated by anyone provided with the necessary knowledge and equipment. The explanatory power of the latter depends on 'abduction to the best explanation' from information acquired from history. Nevertheless, this can provide reasonable confidence in the reliability of historical reports by employing other criteria for the calculation of probability.

The probability of the existence of God and the probability of divine revelation as well as other aspects of religious belief have been discussed at length by Richard Swinburne who calculates such probabilities using Bayes's theorem.[3] Although the calculation of probability for historical events does not compare closely with the calculation of probability in scientific experiments, it is still a valuable way of quantifying probability for the events of history which, of course, cannot be repeated.

---

3. Richard Swinburne makes use of the calculus of probability and Bayes's theorem to assess the probability of theism in *The Existence of God* second edition (Oxford: Clarendon Press, 2004), 329–341, of revelation in *Revelation: From Metaphor to Analogy* second edition (Oxford: University Press, 2007), 345–356, of Jesus being God incarnate who rose from the dead in *The Resurrection of God Incarnate*, (Oxford: Clarendon Press, 2003), 204-215 and in *Epistemic Justification* (Oxford: Clarendon Press, 2001), chapters 3 and 4.

Atheism, a belief that there is no god to account for what exists, is a common belief. But a commitment to this belief must also consider the evidence provided by the life of a man who appeared in history in order to reveal God and his plans and purposes. His display of knowledge and extraordinary capabilities were characteristics never seen in an ordinary human being before him or since and make him worthy of note. Uncertainty about there being 'something out there' referring to some kind of a god or power needs to consider the evidence of this unique man and the kind of god he revealed.

Believing something to be true and 'believing in' someone conveys different nuances. Believing in someone conveys the idea of trust. This tends to carry the activity of believing beyond intellectual assent and into the realm of interpersonal relationships. Nevertheless, trust is usually a response to that which is believed by intellectual assent. Belief in Jesus Christ demands this kind of trust when the evidence of his life is examined.

God's revelation for Christian belief is generally confined to the biblical writings. However, a god who possesses unimaginable capability could reasonably be expected to have contributed in some way providentially to the discovery by human beings of the way in which he has made the universe. This kind of revelation suggests that science and theology are complementary in their provision of understanding. In many instances the application of scientific explanations to theological hypotheses tends to increase confidence in the truth of some theological claims. An obvious example is a belief in the existence of God, a belief which may be inferred by the observation of a physical universe which cannot self-create, and the observed consistency of the natural laws which govern its functions. In the New Testament record the apostle Paul appeals to this kind of evidence,

> God's invisible qualities . . . his eternal power and divine nature (θειότης, divinity)—have been clearly seen, being understood from what he has made (Rom 1:20).

In discussing Jesus' ontology in this investigation some scientific knowledge is used to clarify theology.

The Christian religion is based on biblical revelation which has come largely through selected people, prophets and apostles, and in historical increments in narratives. This method can make the interpretation of God's revelation and motives sometimes unclear. Therefore, some difficulties are encountered in seeking to comprehend the coming into the world of one who claimed to have emerged from God as God's son in Jn 16:28,

> ἐξῆλθον παρὰ τοῦ πατρὸς καὶ ἐλήλυθα εἰς τὸν κόσμον,
> (I have emerged from the Father and have come into the world).

A methodology for emerging from God and arriving in the world could provide support for belief in such a statement and action.

The title 'Son of God' has been used by Christians for centuries and has been usually reserved for Jesus of Nazareth, especially when the adjective μονγενής, (only-begotten), is stipulated. This specific use of sonship is considered traditionally to have a metaphorical meaning rather than a literal one. Although this distinction is not generally made, Charles Sherlock among few others explicitly notes a lack of literality in this sonship, otherwise he feels, 'if the son had a beginning in time, he must be a creature, wholly separate from God'.[4] I will propose that this is not necessarily a valid conclusion, as will be explained in the course of this investigation.

The sonship of Jesus is thought to be definitely not biological in the sense that it did not come about by sexual intercourse between a male and a female human being. The traditional concept of theologians is the existence of a second eternal divine individual, referred to as an *hypostasis* or person besides God, who is designated 'Son of God' and who somehow became incarnate.[5] Such belief seems contradictory to monotheism, a belief inherited by Christians from the Hebrew religion. However, this contradiction is overlooked or called a mystery. These concepts require further investigation.

This idea of sonship which was devised by theologians of the early centuries regarding a second pre-existent deity is far removed from the simple statements found in the New Testament narrative. One motive for this may be to differentiate this sonship from those generally believed by ancient people to have resulted from their

---

4. Charles Sherlock, *God on the Inside: Trinitarian Spirituality* (Canberra: Acorn Press, 1991), 52.
5. Donald A Carson, *Jesus the Son of God: A Christological Title Often Overlooked, Sometimes Misunderstood, and Currently Disputed* (Wheaton, Illinois: Crossway, 2012) traces the 'trajectories' of the term and finds that they lead to Jesus.

gods who supposedly had sexual relations with humans. Yet Jesus' conception and birth involved real biology since God's son arrived by pregnancy and he was delivered like any other human baby. While a miraculous conception is claimed, the mechanism for this remains obscure. Therefore, a methodology is proposed for Jesus' coming and it is sought in the biblical record and in scientific understanding.

The biblical revelation in existence in documents is believed by this writer among others to have come ultimately from God inspiring human beings. This is not assumed without evidence, since the writers of the documents or their sources were enabled by God to perform miraculous works which God alone could bring about.

This suggests the endorsement of God for their writings. At the same time, it is considered that the understanding of such revelation needs to be examined in its original language as far as possible, and by taking into consideration the contexts in which it is expressed. Even with the application of these requirements, theological language alone may not adequately explain the revelation of God about the coming of his son. Modern knowledge from science is found helpful in identifying a methodology for his coming.

A fictitious god fathering an offspring by sexual intercourse with a human was an acceptable belief in Graeco-Roman mythology. But the genuine God is also believed to have fathered a son, miraculously rather than sexually, with a woman for the purpose of saving his people from their sins (Mt 1:21). However, some kind of change in God is required in order to father a material offspring. This, however, runs contrary to perceptions about God who is considered to be unchangeable spirit. This unchangeability in God becomes a sticking point for theological understanding regarding the Son's origin. An interpretation of God's unchangeability in the biblical record is sometimes confused with God's constancy. The latter is assured in that even if the whole creation wears out like an old garment, God remains unchanged or constant, σὺ δὲ αὐτός εἶ (Ps 102:25–27 LXX), (but you remain the same).

Such steadfastness has been interpreted as being an attribute of 'immutability', an inability or perhaps unwillingness by God to change in his being, perfections, purposes and promises, according to Louis Berkhof.[6] But in order to maintain an attribute of immutability

---

6. Louis Berkhof, *Systematic Theology* (Grand Rapids: Eerdmans, 1939, 1941), 58–59.

in a transcendent God, a metaphorical sonship has been suggested for Jesus rather than a literal one. Louis Berkhof's solution for the dilemma is that 'the incarnation brought no change in the Being . . . of God, for it was his eternal good pleasure to send the Son of his love into the world'. This suggests a constancy of purpose rather than denying an ontological change. However, the traditional theological position continues to believe in the pre-existence of an eternal son who was subject to change and was sent into the world as a human being.

The writing that follows contemplates a unique change undertaken by God in his spiritual substance in order to father an offspring who was born into the world. This event prompted the writers of the Nicene Creed (CE 325) to describe the offspring as

> Γεννηθέντα ἐκ τοῦ πατρὸς μονογενῆ, τοῦτ' ἔστιν ἐκ οὐσίας πατρός
> Lines 6, 7, (Born of the father as the only-begotten, that is out of the substance of the Father).[7]

The coming of Jesus of Nazareth into the world has ignited many debates concerning his origin, the method of his arrival and his nature. These have an influence on his adequacy to be the saviour of humankind. His reported miraculous activities and his alleged resurrection from the dead have challenged the assumption that he was a mere human being and have suggested that he was also divine.

Despite some doubts concerning the reliability of the available reports about him, examination of the ancient documents supports the likelihood that events involving him were witnessed and generally reported accurately. Disbelieving these, some have even suggested that the reports were fictitious stories made up to influence the credulous. A claim that he was an idealised imaginary man to be emulated 'can be decisively refuted without once appealing to Christian evidence'.[8] Jesus is mentioned by Graeco-Roman and Jewish sources, a notable one being the well-known non-Christian Jewish historian Josephus who identifies Jesus in his time. He writes,

---

7. T Herbert Bindley, *The Oecumenical Documents of the Faith* fourth edition, revised by FW Green (London: Methuen & Co Ltd, 1950), 26.
8. Craig L Blomberg, *Jesus and the Gospels* (Leister: Apollos, 1997), 370.

> Now, there was about this time, Jesus, a wise man, if it be lawful to call him a man, for he was a doer of wonderful works .... He was [the] Christ; and when Pilate, at the suggestion of the principal men among us, had condemned him to the cross, those that loved him at the first did not forsake him, for he appeared to them alive again the third day...[9]

Even if it is the case that Josephus' writing was 'edited' by later Christians, a claim suggested by the 'christianisation' of the writing above, the mention of Jesus by Josephus is adequate evidence of at least his existence at that time.

Religious language has understandably involved metaphorical and figurative concepts in order to express aspects of reality. It is almost incredible to imagine a great spiritual God who created a vast universe desiring to have relationship with human creatures and to communicate with them. To overcome this difficulty in human perception, God has sometimes been imagined in finite 'anthropomorphic' terms. For example, God's lordship over all is envisaged as that which has been seen in a historical king enthroned, dressed in royal garments and wearing a crown. Although similar 'anthropomorphisms' can be helpful, they may lead to perceptions which consider God to be a human being unless one pauses consciously to consider the reality to which reference is made.

In all fields of knowledge intellectual satisfaction and confidence depend on the perception of the reality of claims and their supportive evidence. Reality may be thought of as the property of something or someone or some event being substantial, actual or objective. Spiritual concepts which are not readily recognised by the physical senses also require evidence which is perceived by one's thought. Austin Farrer expresses the importance of accessing reality in theology by asserting that *Reality is a nuisance to those who want to make it up as they go along.*[10]

A biblical example is provided by the early Christian Stephen who engaged with reality with fatal consequences when he challenged

---

9. 'Antiquities of the Jews', in *Josephus: Complete Works,* translated by William Whiston (Grand Rapids, Michigan: Kregel Publications, 1978), Book XVIII, chapter III. 3, page 379.
10. Austin Farrer, *Saving Belief: A Discussion of Essentials* (London: Hodder and Stoughton, 1964), 33–34.

conventional belief. He expressed the reality conveyed by the Christ event in contrast to belief in figurative aspects of the Law and the temple. He points out, (Acts 7:48) 'However, the Most High does not live in houses made by men'. And he quotes God's words in Isaiah 66:1, 2, 'Heaven is my throne and earth is my footstool ... Has not my hand made all these things?'

The response of Malcolm Jeeves to Farrer's statement is insightful. He claims that *Reality is indeed a nuisance, but it is all we have—and we do well to pay attention to it unless we wish to live in a world of fantasy and wishful thinking.*[11] The reality associated with science is noted by Paul R Gross and Norman Levitt who observe that *Science succeeds precisely because it has accepted a bargain in which even the boldest imagination stands hostage to reality.*[12] Therefore, it is important to know the reality to which various forms of expression such as metaphor and *synecdoche*, so common in biblical writings, make reference.

The plan of this investigation is to introduce in Chapter one some basic epistemic background which is thought to be useful for the claims made in later chapters. Chapter two provides evidence for the belief that Jesus was indeed human, and Chapter three that he was also divine. Much of this evidence is provided by the testimony of the biblical record written by believers, and therefore it may be thought to have considerable bias. This in itself does not make it untrue, given the ethical behaviour demonstrated by the highly ethical man, Jesus, who influenced his followers to have integrity in all their ways. Mistaken they may have been, but not deliberately deceptive. As noted, God's approval of them is evidenced by miraculous works.

Chapter four provides a methodology, to a considerable extent technical and scientific but simplified, for the most likely way in which Jesus could be human and divine. In this section, some long-held beliefs of method are shown to be inadequate, and some very modern methods are also shown to be untenable. Consequent upon this methodology, Chapter five provides biblical evidence for God's literal fatherhood of Jesus, and Chapter six discusses some objections which could be brought against the methodology proposed because

---

11. Malcolm Jeeves, editor, *From Cells to Souls and Beyond: Changing Portraits of Human Nature* (Grand Rapids: Eerdmans, 2004), 233.
12. Paul R Gross and Norman Levitt, *Higher Superstition*, (Baltimore: John Hopkins University Press, 1994), 234.

of the pre-supposed individual, 'hypostatic', pre-existence of Jesus. Finally, Chapter seven considers the logical implications for the doctrine of the Trinity if the proposed methodology is correct.

God being spirit does not ontologically possess gender. However, in the ancient writings God has been called 'the father', especially by Jesus who seemed to have an unusually profound depth of knowledge. In this writing it will be proposed that this genderless God was, in reality, Jesus' literal father. Therefore, the title will continue to be used, as well as the masculine pronoun to refer to God.[13] English translations are generally my own and tend to be more literal than those found in translated Bibles. The Greek text in ancient writings hopefully helps to make the original wording readily available for those who wish to check it.

---

13. A balanced view of the use of gender is presented by Charles Sherlock, *God on the Inside*, chapter six.

Chapter Two
Evidence for the Humanity of Jesus

Apart from an alleged angelic appearance to the chosen mother and one in a dream to the assumed father, both recounted publically years later, there was no indication at the birth of Jesus that God was genetically involved in the ontology of the baby born at Bethlehem to Mary and Joseph of Nazareth. An angelic announcement to shepherds, prophecies accompanying his presentation at the temple and a special visit by Magi from the East referred to the child as a future significant figure, a king or messiah, without suggesting divinity in his ontology. Jesus appeared to have grown up like any other boy in a village and worked most of his life as a carpenter helping to support the family which included brothers and sisters. His appearance and way of life had all the marks of an ordinary human being. But his witnessed miraculous activity and his resurrection from the dead indicated that this human being may have been also divine.

However, the fact that Jesus actually died and the physiological processes which led to his death leave no doubt as to his genuine humanity. Whether by natural means or by trauma, death results from the failure of physiological processes designed to keep the body alive, and these failed in Jesus as they did in other crucified men. So his genuine humanity may be confidently deduced by the physiology at work during the process of dying on a cross.

But the biblical narrative describes Jesus on the cross as bowing his head and giving up his spirit.[1] This, coupled with his claim that no one could take his life, that he had power to lay it down and power

---

1. Matthew 27:50 ἀφῆκεν τὸ πνεῦμα, (dismissed the spirit), John 19:30 παρέδωκεν τὸ πνεῦμα, (he surrendered the spirit), Mark 15:37 and Luke 23:46 ἐξέπνευσεν, (expired).

to take it up again (Jn 10:18), has been interpreted as some kind of convenient suicide. John Wilkinson affirms that Jesus 'died because he willed to die'.[2] This assertion could be interpreted as there being no natural patho-physiological mechanism involved in his death and that he simply decided the moment he wished to die and gave up his spirit. A quasi-suicidal method of dying seems to make him less human than the rest of humanity. RO Ball states, 'If men have not the power, apart from suicide, to choose the moment of death, then Jesus did not experience death as men know it'. Therefore, to suggest that 'he was able, voluntarily to surrender his life is to suggest that while he was not prepared to come down from the cross he was willing to escape it (his suffering) another way'.

K Leese adds a medical opinion, that 'even the voluntary surrender of life must involve neuro-chemical changes'.[3] I suggest that the most likely meaning of his giving up and taking up his life again is a reference to his surrender to the executing authorities resulting in his death and his expected resurrection, rather than to the overriding of physiological processes.

The Natural Method of Jesus' Dying

Crucifixion was a dreaded means of execution and was designed not only to kill but also to torture. The experience of thousands of crucifixions informed the Romans, probably by accident, that the confirmation of death on the cross was the flow of some watery liquid as well as blood from the victim's side when it was pierced. The necessity for such confirmation was because no one was permitted to be taken down from the cross alive. The following description of physiological processes and the cause of the described flow of 'blood and water' are necessarily detailed because they differ from previous theories for the way Jesus died.

A claim that Jesus did not really die on the cross but simply fainted and recovered in the cool of the cave tomb and walked out was motivated by his reported resurrection. Barbara Thiering makes this

---

2. John Wilkinson, 'The Physical Cause of the Death of Christ', in *The Expository Times*, 83 (1971): 104–107.
3. In reply to Wilkinson, *The Expository Times*, 83 (1972): 248, 'Physical Cause of the Death of Jesus: (1) RO Ball, A Theological Comment, (2) K Leese, A Medical Opinion'.

assumption from John 19:34, considering that Jesus was alive when a soldier cut him with a spear when he was thought to be dead on the cross because he bled. Therefore it is assumed that he must have been taken down from the cross alive and he reappeared to his followers.[4] Similar beliefs have been held throughout history.

In order to provide evidence that Jesus had indeed died on the cross, and hence to provide support for a real resurrection, a number of Christian medical personnel have sought to describe the most likely physiological means by which Jesus had died. The descriptions of such methods of dying have been proposed since the late nineteenth century and some have been summarised by John Wilkinson.[5] His treatment of the subject has been accepted by modern commentators.[6]

Though Wilkinson omits Brown's least traumatic use of the spear, a nudge to see if the apparently dead Jesus would flinch,[7] he rejects Creighton's theory of a blister on the skin, giving rise to blood and water,[8] and Haughton's theory that blood originated from the lung and water from the pericardium.[9] Other theories rightly rejected are the *broken heart* made popular by Stroud, suggesting that the heart muscle ruptured into the pericardium, and as blood and serum separated, it gave the appearance of blood and water.[10] Almost similar is Barbet's theory, proposing a stab in the heart giving rise to blood and *water* from a pericardial effusion.[11] Sava's suggestion of bleeding into the pleural cavity after which blood red cells and serum separated and appeared at the spear wound seems to describe

---

4. Barbara Thiering, *Jesus the Man* (Sydney: Doubleday, 1992), 420, fn 9.
5. John Wilkinson, 'The Incident of the Blood and Water in John 19:34', in the *Scottish Journal of Theology,* 28 (1975): 149–172.
6. Craig S Keener, *The Gospel of John: A Commentary,* in 2 volumes (Massachusetts: Hendrickson Publishers, 2003), 1153, fn 754 and Craig L Blomberg, *The Historical Reliability of John's Gospel* (Leicester: Apollos, 2001), 255, fn 378.
7. Raymond E Brown, *The Gospel According to John,* 2 volumes, (Garden City: Doubleday, 1966, 1967), 935.
8. C Creighton, "Cross" in *Encyclopaedia Biblica* (London: A and C Black, 1914).
9. S Haughton, *The Speaker's Commentary on the New Testament,* Edited by F C Cook, (London: John Murray, 1881), Volume 4, 349, 350.
10. William Stroud, *The physical Cause of the Death of Christ,* Revised second edition, (London: Hamilton and Adams, 1871), 73–80.
11. P Barbet, *The Passion of our Lord Jesus Christ,* translated from the French by The Earl of Wicklow (Dublin: Clonmore and Reynolds Ltd, 1954), 100.

a similar process.¹² Water from a dilated stomach and blood from intra-thoracic blood vessels was a theory proposed by J. L. Cameron and popularised by A. R. Short, but is also unlikely,¹³ as is the theory of Primrose advocating a lower abdominal wound.¹⁴

The hypothesis which satisfies Wilkinson consists of a modification of two views, those of Haughton and Barbet. He concludes that as the soldier thrust his spear deeply and widely into the Lord's thoracic side, it first penetrated the lung and, being waved around, cut across some of the larger vessels at the root of the lung. Blood flowed into the wound and appeared on the surface of the chest. The spear then passed further inwards and penetrated the pericardial sac, which contained an increased quantity of fluid produced by the stress of the foregoing scourging. This was released and appeared on the body surface as water. Almost all of the theories listed have similarities to Wilkinson's, and locate the stab wound of the spear into the thorax. Modern movie films depicting Christ's crucifixion show a spear flung at Jesus' chest and blood and water spurting from the site of penetration.

I suggest that the medical authors have followed a *syncretism* for the meaning of the word πλευρά, 'pleura' (side). The dictionary meaning of the Greek word is rib or side. Of some interest is the coincidence of the transliterated word 'pleura' with the current anatomical name of the thin membrane lining the inside of the thorax, 'the parietal pleura', and also lines the surface of lungs, 'the visceral pleura'. This may have had a coincidental influence on medical personel in drawing attention to the side of the thorax. But the cardiovascular changes taking place in a man dying on a cross suggest that the injury made by the spear was anatomically elsewhere.

The upright position of the crucified person, the head being uppermost, leads to pooling of blood in the parts of the body below the

---

12. AF Sava, 'The Wound in the Side of Christ', *The Catholic Biblical Quarterly,* 19 (1954): 344.
13. Quoted by Randolph VG Tasker, *John: An Introductory Commentary,* Tyndale New Testament Commentaries, General Editor Randolph VG Tasker (London: The Tyndale Press, 1953), 96. Cameron read 'How Our Lord Died' to the Third International Congress of Catholic Doctors at Lisbon in June 1947.
14. WB Primrose, 'A Surgeon Looks at the Crucifixion', in *Hibbert Journal,* 47 (1949): 382–388.

level of the heart. This results in lowering the blood pressure because less blood returns to the heart through the large vein, the Inferior Vena Cava. Therefore, less blood is pumped out to all parts of the body needing oxygen. To compensate for this, the heart rate increases and contractions of the heart muscle strengthen automatically (or more precisely 'autonomically', referring to the autonomic or involuntary nervous system which governs these changes).

For this to be effective, there must be sufficient blood returning to the heart and this is done by tensing the leg muscles voluntarily by standing on a foot-shelf on the cross onto which the feet were nailed. This activity results in the flow of venous blood through veins supplied with unidirectional valves and empty into the Inferior Vena Cava. From there blood proceeds upwards to the heart. In addition, increased inspiratory activity in depth and frequency helps to exert 'suction' of blood towards the heart from lower regions by decreasing the pressure within the thorax.

These compensatory actions maintain cardiac output for a considerable amount of time, allowing crucifixion to last up to several days as a means of torture. In order to hasten the process of dying, for example because the Sabbath was approaching, the legs of the crucified were broken resulting in shock by blood being shed into the tissues of the legs. It also eliminates to a considerable extent the venous return to the heart by abolishing a major compensating factor, the tensing of the legs. This allows the crucified to die more quickly.

The act of mercy or convenience was carried out on two of the victims, but when it was about to be performed on Jesus, he was apparently already dead. The speed of this death was somewhat surprising, but a victim could not be released for burial without evidence that death had ensued. Therefore, the spear was thrust into his side by a soldier accustomed to these kinds of executions in order to test for the occurrence of death by the appearance of the expected watery liquid.

Ball's suggestion of a convenient suicide may be answered by a combination of events preceding Jesus' crucifixion and his attitude to his impending death. Jesus' suffering in custody, a sleepless night accompanied by physical taunting (Lk 22:63–65 and parallels.) followed by judicial trials, and a pre-crucifixion scourging (Mt 27:26 and parallels) contributed to physical weakness as evidenced by his requiring help to carry part of the cross (Lk 23:26 and parallels). In addition to his weakened state, being assured that his death was in the will of God, Jesus relaxed rather than trying to prolong life as long as possible. If he did not perform voluntary compensatory actions such as tensing and straightening his legs and taking deep inspiratory breaths to aid venous return to the heart, then he allowed nature to take its course resulting in his death. In this respect he gave up struggling to stay alive rather than actively ending his life.

Near death, the heart would be beating at its maximal effective rate and at its maximal contractility. However, eventually all 'automatic' compensatory processes would be ineffectual and the heart would stop, resulting in death. In view of this, at death the heart would contain almost no blood, this being pooled in the Inferior Vena Cava in the abdomen. This is the largest vein in the body and collects blood from the legs and abdominal organs. Its course begins at a horizontal level just below and to the right of the navel, proceeds upwards along the right side of the vertebral column and ends in the heart just above the diaphragm at a level behind the lower end of the sternum.

When the heart stops, this long vertical tube filled with blood remains immobile and the blood within it begins to undergo sedimentation, the cells settling to the bottom of the column while the plasma remains in the upper part of the vein. Sedimentation tends to occur more rapidly in situations of dehydration and shock in which circulating blood volume is reduced, being pooled in the lower regions of the body due to hanging on a cross for several hours. This was applicable to Jesus and led to increased aggregation of red cells resulting in a more rapid sedimentation rate than is expected in an unstressed person. Therefore, after two to three hours of immobility approximately the lower half of the column in the vertical vein would consist of red blood and the upper half would be clear plasma. The blood would not coagulate during this time because the vein itself had not been injured, as the clotting of blood requires 'injury factors' from the containing vessel in order to commence.

Philological Evidence for Citing the Speared Side

The meaning of 'side' requires clarification because of its influence on opinions which drew attention to a thoracic wound and continue to do so. The most helpful writers of antiquity using the word *pleura* to mean ribs and sides of the body, as opposed to geographical sides which use the same word, have been Hippocrates (fifth century BCE) and Galen (second century CE). Rufus (first century CE) has been helpful in applying alternative words for anatomical sites. The majority of references by Hippocrates and Galen to πλευραί are to ribs in the plural. This may be due to a preoccupation with ailments which plagued people at the time, such as pulmonary tuberculosis and which drew attention to the chest. Although references to the abdomen are comparatively few, they are unmistakeable when the context in which they are mentioned is considered. It is noted as a tendency rather than to be claimed as a rule that references to the singular use of the word 'pleura', side, generally mean the abdominal side.

Rufus defined πλευρόν, (side), the neuter singular equivalent of the feminine singular πλευρά, as πᾶν τὸ ὑπὸ τῇ μασχάλῃ (everything below the armpit).[15] As a border between the thorax and abdomen are situated the cartilages, χόνδροι . . . τὰ πέρατα τῶν πλευρῶν τῶν νόθων, (the parts beyond the false ribs). By this he means the cartilages which join the lower ribs together in front rather than a reference to the last two ribs on each side which have taken the name 'false' currently. These cartilages separate the thorax with the ribs from the abdomen. Below the cartilages are the 'hypochondria', singular 'hypochondrium', ὑποχόνδρια . . . τὰ ὑπὸ τοῖς χόνδροις μυώδη, (the hypochondria . . . . the muscles below the cartilages). This refers to the uppermost part of the lateral abdominal wall, which has muscles, but no bones or cartilages.

Although the commonest use of 'pleura', particularly in the plural, refers to ribs, in the following contexts it is used to mean the side of the abdomen. This is due to the mention with the word πλευρά, 'pleura', (side), of processes that can occur only in the abdomen, such as abdominal pain, diarrhoea and the mention of bile. The full Greek text is omitted from the reference if it is felt that it does not contribute to the understanding of the information provided.

1. A clear reference is made by Hippocrates,

> A frothy scum on bilious stools, (χολώδεσι διαχωρήμασι), is a bad sign, especially in a person with diarrhoea and who had pain in his loins beforehand. Intermittent pains in the side, (πλευρόν), in such cases are a sign of derangement of the mind, (παραφροσύνην σημαίνει).[16]

---

15. Rufus Ephesius Med. TLG, *De Corporis Humani Appellationibus*, 89. 1-115. 1.
16. *Hippocrates*, edited and translated by Paul Potter, Volume VIII, Prorrhetic I, (Cambridge, Massachusetts: Harvard University Press, 1995), 21–22.

Although today we would consider his conclusion about derangement of the mind doubtful, πλευρόν here obviously refers to the abdominal, rather than the thoracic side because the pathological process is an abdominal one, accompanied by diarrhoea. The mention of πλευρόν in the singular is unusual in the Hippocratic writings, the plural being preferred when referring to ribs, while the singular here is referring to the abdominal side.

2. From Prorrhetic I. 140-146 the abdominal cavity, (κοιλία), is mentioned three times and 'hypochondrium' twice. The process is accompanied by jaundice, thus involving the liver or biliary system in the abdomen. In 146,

> Yellowish stools with small sticky pieces, (Αἱ πυκναὶ καὶ κατὰ μικρὰ ἐπαναστάσιες ὑπόξανθο), passed frequently a little at a time, in association with pains in the hypochondrium and the side, (μετὰ ὑποχονδρίου ἀλγήματος καὶ πλευροῦ ἱκτεριώδεες), are a sign of jaundice.

It is noted again that the side, πλευροῦ, 'pleurou', is in the singular genetive case.

3. A further use of πλευροῦ in the singular meaning 'of the side' in Hippocrates is found in biliary disease in the abdomen,

> When pains in the side, (πλευροῦ ἀλγήματα), associated with bilious spitting disappear without any reason patients become delirious.[17]

4. In several situations Hippocrates uses two abdominal sites which run together as a phrase. This is 'hypochondria and sides'. He recommends a clinical observation, whether the hypochondria and sides, (ὑποχόνδρια καὶ πλευρά) (the plural neuter form of πλευρόν, both in the plural and referring to the right and left abdominal sides), are without pain or feel hot or are held crookedly or look swollen or full. There is also instruction for an aperient, and that the bowel action should be noted if it is clear or black.[18] The problem discussed is undoubtedly abdominal. The

---

17. *Hippocrates,*, 97.
18. Hippocrates, *TLG* 'De Diaeta Acutorum' 9. 5-14.

ὑποχόνδρια καὶ πλευρά (hypochondria and sides), are adjacent regions of the abdomen, the sides being situated just below and lateral to the 'hypochondria'. The same phrase, associating the abdominal sides with the hypochondria, is mentioned by Hippocrates in De diaeta acutorum 23.7, and in Epistulae 21.29, and in similar words by Galen.[19]

5. Galen, more than any other writer refers to Hippocrates, at times quoting him verbatim. Galen often calls the abdominal sides λαγόνας, (lagonas), but sometimes πλευρά, 'pleura', the region below the 'false ribs' which consists of the soft lateral part of the abdomen.[20]

> When there has been faecal material sequestered in the intestines, that is, without bowel actions for a long time, of necessity there will be damage to the side, (ἀναγκαῖον ἐστι βλάβην γενέσθαι τῇ πλευρᾷ) διὰ τὴν ἔμφραξιν τῶν ἐντέρων, (through the blockage of the intestines).[21]

The reference to the side here can be none other than to the abdominal side.

6. Galen recommends a drink of honey and vinegar, given for pain, and suggests that it be given in small quantities, and it be given cold in summer and warm in winter. It is given in small quantities

> so that by the time it reaches the stomach, it becomes warm, before it loses its coolness by the time it reaches the side (ὡς ἂν ἐν τῇ γαστρὶ φθάνον χλιανθῆναι πρὶν διαδοθῆναι τὴν ἐξ αὐτοῦ ψύξιν ἄχριτῆς πλευρᾶς).[22]

As previously, the word for side, πλευρᾶς, (of the side), is in the singular and can mean only the abdominal side because of the mention of the stomach. As indicated above, a rule may not be drawn from these few observations, but the word again is in the singular suggesting a trend that 'side' in the singular is more likely to refer to the abdominal side than to the thorax.

---

19. Galen, *TLG*, 'In Hippocratis de victa acutorum commentaria', iv, 15. 822.
20. Galen, *TLG*, 'De Usu Partium, 3.322.6; 3.397.4
21. Galen, *TLG*, 'In Hippocratis de victa acutorum commentaria' IV 15. 486.6.
22. Galen, *TLG*, 'In Hippocratis de victa acutorum commentaria', IV 15. 501.1.

It is concluded from this brief word search that Jn 19:34 τὴν πλευρὰ ἔνυξεν, (he pierced the side) uses the word πλευρά, 'pleura' (side) to situate the wound inflicted by the soldier's spear in the abdominal side. Considering this with the physiological evidence for the method of dying on a cross, it seems certain that the right abdominal side of Jesus was pierced. The spear would have travelled beneath the liver at a level where the column of liquid in the vein would be red blood rather than plasma. It would penetrate deeply to be stopped by the vertebral column, opening the Inferior Vena Cava, and releasing first a quantity of red blood, perhaps fifty to one hundred millilitres. For this to find its way to the exterior, the spear had to remain *in situ*, with its flange at the layer of muscles and skin to maintain an opening, otherwise the contents of the vein would have dispersed into the abdominal cavity unobserved. Immediately following the blood, there would flow the same volume of plasma descending from above the level of the red blood, from the upper part of the vein. The flange of the spear at the abdominal wall would allow the clear liquid to flow to the surface and provide evidence to the soldier that death had supervened. The whole process would take seconds.

This has been a discussion of interest to few readers, but hopefully it settles a historical detail. The piercing the side of the crucified was a process well known to executioners and was not a means of killing the victim, but a means of ascertaining that death had already supervened. It is likely that the process was also carried out on the other victims without being mentioned. The practice was probably so common that it did not require comment in the literature. However, Quintilian writes, 'victims could be given for burial once they were pierced'.[23] Therefore, Jesus died on the cross and was buried dead, and his alleged resurrection was a reality.

The Meaning of the Flow of Blood and Water from Jesus' Side

The immediate meaning of the flow of blood and water from Jesus' side was that he was dead and could be taken down from the cross

---

23. Quintilian, *The Institution Oratoria*, in 4 volumes, Translated by HE Butler, LCL, (London: Heineman, 1969), 6.9. Also Raymond E Brown *The Death of the Messiah: From Gethsemane to the Grave: A Commentary on the Passion Narrative in the Four Gospels*, in 2 volumes (New York: Doubleday, 1994), 1177, fn 91.

and be entombed. However, fifty or more years later when the fourth Gospel was probably written the event attained a more significant theological meaning.

Although the humanity of Jesus is evident in the physiological means by which his death occurred, it did not detract from his concurrent divinity. For John both the humanity and the divinity of Jesus must be maintained together much as the blood and the water flowed together, even though the latter had an analogical meaning.

The incident is described in John 19:34, 35.

> εἷς τῶν στρατιωτῶν λόγχῃ αὐτοῦ τὴν πλευρὰν ἔνυξεν, καὶ ἐξῆλθεν εὐθὺς αἷμα καὶ ὕδωρ (one of the soldiers pierced his side with his spear and immediately flowed out blood and water)

But the next verse emphasises what was witnessed and the reason for the emphasis is that the readers might believe.

> καὶ ὁ ἑωρακὼς μεμαρτύρηκεν, καὶ ἀληθινὴ αὐτοῦ ἐστιν ἡ μαρτυρία, καὶ ἐκεῖνος οἶδεν ὅτι ἀληθῆ λέγει, ἵνα καὶ ὑμεῖς πιστεύσητε, (and the one who watched has borne witness and his witness is true, and he knows that he tells the truth, so that you may believe.)

What was to be believed was not merely that the flow of blood and water meant that death had occurred because this was common knowledge. At this point in time he wanted his readers to believe in Jesus' divinity as well as his humanity.

Craig Keener rightly states that in his Gospel John is interested in interpreting, and not merely reporting, his observation. Similarly, Raymond E Brown recognises that John's intention in recording the flow of blood and water is theological.[24] Granted this to be the case, there is no unanimity among scholars as to the theological meaning which was intended by the author. A number of interpretations have been offered, but the three most plausible will be considered. These are the 'anti-docetic polemic', the 'symbolism of the Spirit', and an 'entirely divine Jesus' in the fourth Gospel.

An 'anti-docetic polemic' in the blood and water defends the real humanity of Jesus against any idea of Docetism which denied it. It is

---

24. Craig Keener, *The Gospel of John*, 1152. RE Brown *The Death of the Messiah*, 1179.

favoured by Donald Carson and George R Beasley-Murray. Carson considers that there were already, at the time of writing the Gospel, docetic influences at work in the church. These became much more pronounced by the time the Epistles of John were written as suggested in 1 John 2:22, 4:1–4, 5:6–9. Carson also records that the human body was thought at the time to consist of blood and water.[25]

Beasley-Murray refers to J Blinzler's purpose for the spearing, 'that he should not have a spark of life when taken down from the cross'. Beasley-Murray believes that the evangelist wanted his readers to recognize the reality of the death of Jesus, and so the reality of his humanity, as a 'man of flesh and blood'.[26] However, as noted above, the purpose of the spearing was not to kill, but to ensure that death had already taken place.

The anti-docetic intention of the evangelist is also acknowledged by JH Bernard and Frederick F Bruce.[27] However, Stephen Smalley believes that docetic Gnosticism was still at an early and developing stage at the time that John wrote the Gospel. He believes that the evangelist was preoccupied with Christology, but not with Docetism which emerged as a later problem.[28]

Blood and water as 'symbolic of the Spirit' given through the death of Christ is advocated by Brown and Keener, and it is claimed to be

---

25. Donald A Carson, *The Gospel According to John* (Leicester: InterVarsity Press, 1991), 623, 624. Also G Richter, *Studiem zum Johannesevangelium* (Regensburg: Verlag Friedrich Puster, 1977), 125. In addition, JH Bernard, *The Gospel According to St. John,* In two volumes (Edinburgh: T&T Clark, 1922), 2:647. Rudolf Bultmann, *The Gospel of John: A Commentary* (Oxford: Blackwell, 1971), 678, fn 1.
26. George R Beasley-Murray, *John,* Word Biblical Commentary, 36 (Waco, Texas: Word Books, 1987), 356. J Blinzler, *The Trial of Jesus: The Jewish and Roman Proceedings Against Jesus Christ Described and Asserted from the Oldest Accounts,* translated by Isabel and Florence McHugh (Westminster: Newman, 1959), 391.
27. JH Bernard, *A Critical and Exegetical Commentary on the Gospel According to St. John,* edited by AH McNeil, in 2 volumes (Edinburgh: T&T Clark, 1922), 2:647. Frederick F Bruce, *The Gospel of John: Introduction, Exposition and Notes* (Grand Rapids: Eerdmans, 1983), 376.
28. Stephen S Smalley, *John: Evangelist & Interpreter,* second edition (Downers Grove, Illinois: InterVarsity Press, 1998), 171, 172.

the most common scholarly view.[29] Keener believes that the primary emphasis of the event of the flow of blood and water is the anomaly of water. Blood would be expected to flow from a spear wound, but not water. To Keener, the theological significance of this 'is clear enough in the context of the entire Gospel'.

It is claimed that water has great symbolic value in the Gospel, exhibiting a motif that runs through it (1:31, 33, 2: 6, 3:5, 4:14, 5:2, 9:7, and 13:5). But its primary theological exposition is found in 7:37-39, about the rivers of living water. It is thought that the water motif climaxes at the cross, where water flows from Jesus' side. It is suggested that now that Jesus has been glorified (7:39) in his death and resurrection and ascension, the Spirit of life flows from him to those who trust him (7:37). Brown makes the same symbolic interpretation in the flow of blood and water. Jesus' death is signified by the blood, and the promised Spirit flowing from within him is signified by the water. Other less plausible suggestions have been made, but they account for the blood but not for the water.

Paul Haupt claims that Jn 1:18, μονογενὴς θεὸς ὁ ὢν εἰς τὸν κόλπον τοῦ πατρός, (the only-begotten God who is in the bosom of the Father) emphasizes his divine nature. Haupt believes that 'in the Fourth Gospel Jesus is not a human being, but a deity'.[30] In support of this, he refers to an ancient belief which appears to have originated with Homer in the eighth century BCE epic, *The Iliad*.

The background of the event to which reference is made begins in Book 5 (of 24 books), lines 1-330. From there to line 342 Diomedes, a Greek warrior, under instructions from the goddess Athene, hurled a spear, piercing the hand of Aphrodite, a goddess 'without warcraft'. She had come to rescue her son Aeneas, whom she bore to a mortal, Anchises, the son therefore being mortal.

> ... and blood immortal flowed from the goddess, ichor, that which runs in the veins of the blessed divinities; since these eat no food, nor do they drink of the shining wine, and therefore they have no blood and are called immortal.

---

29. Keener, *John*, 1153, n.755, citing M Vellanickal, 'Blood and Water', *Jeevadhara* 8 (1978), 217–230. J McPolin, *John*, New Testament Message 6, (Wilmington: Glazier, 1979), 249. CR Koester, *Symbolism in the Fourth Gospel: Meaning, Mystery, Community* (Minneapolis: Fortress, 1995), 181.
30. Paul Haupt, 'Blood and Water', in *American Journal of Philology*, 45 (1924): 53–55.

Ichor is supposed to be a colourless, perhaps transparent liquid, similar to water. Subsequent writers make mention of this legend. Alexander the Great was quoted as saying when injured by an arrow in battle, 'What flows here, my friends, is blood and not ichor such as flows from the veins of the blessed gods'.[31] Although deities were considered to be immortal, it was dangerous to lose one's *ichor*. The bronze giant Talos, made immortal by Medea, lost all his *ichor* by a nail being taken out of him.[32]

In later times, Celsus (170's CE), mocked the Christians, asking whether Jesus had in his veins the divine liquid that was the blood of the gods. Later still, in defending Christian belief in the deity of Christ, Origen (248 CE) replied to Celsus that from Christ's side flowed pure water, not the *ichor* of the legendary gods.[33]

The idea suggested above, that John used the flow of the water analogically to indicate the divinity of Jesus has interested a number of modern scholars in addition to Haupt, but they mention it only to reject it.[34] Keener argues against this, believing that if one reads this passage outside its Johannine and early Jewish context, one could portray Jesus as a Greek demigod or hero. As this is not the natural way to understand the Gospel, it is rejected. Brown also rejected this view, saying that it was not possible to be certain how John's readers who had a pagan Hellenistic background would understand this event. 'But since nowhere else does John depend on such blatantly pagan imagery to explain Jesus', he could see little reason to suppose that it was a major factor here.[35]

On the other hand, in support of the use of such analogical interpretation, it may be argued that the Gospel was written for both Jews and Gentiles primarily in Asia Minor.[36] The book of the Revelation suggests that John was familiar with the churches in the

---

31. Plutarch, TLG, *Alexander*, 28.3.
32. Apollonius Rhodius, *The Argonautica*, translated by RC Seaton, LCL, (Cambridge: Harvard University Press, 1921), 4. 1679–1680.
33. Origen, *Contra Celsum*, 2.36.
34. Beasley-Murray, *John,* 357; Brown, *John,* 947; Brown, *Death,* 1179; Keener, *John,* 1152.
35. Brown, *Death,* 1179, 1180.
36. Keener, *John,* 146. Irenaeus who had known Polycarp, who had known John, affirms that John was the beloved disciple and wrote in Ephesus, (Irenaeus, *Haer.* 3.1.1). A number of modern scholars also support this view, e. g. Smalley, *John* (2), 76; JC Fenton, *The Gospel According to John in the Revised Standard Version.*

region. Wishing to contextualize his message to the language and thought of the people in that part of the world, John could have used ideas that illustrated the point he wanted to make. Therefore, without believing that there was *ichor* circulating in Jesus' veins, John could have used the event which he had witnessed, the flow of blood and water, to make a point and enunciate a truth which his audience could find applicable from its background. There seems to be no better way than the chosen analogy, to drive home the truth about the humanity and divinity of Jesus Christ.

There is also evidence that the divinity of Jesus came under attack at this time by teaching which denied it. The Ebionites, a Jewish group, considered Jesus to be entirely human.[37]

Any other divinity for them would have meant polytheism. Such views were voiced by Cerinthus who was probably a contemporary of John and living in Ephesus.[38] In order to combat and correct these notions, John appears to have emphasised the divinity of Jesus, assuming his humanity to be obvious.

Although it may be a slight diversion in the discussion, it is highly likely that John wanted to declare the divinity of Jesus as a theme for his Gospel. An attempt to discover a theme for the Gospel of John yields nebulous ideas. The term 'theme' has been used loosely by many writers when more strictly they may have meant 'motif'.[39] However, David Clines suggests a number of characteristics of 'theme' to distinguish it from similar terms, such as 'intention', 'motif', and 'subject', even though it is related to these, because theme relates to larger units than do these other terms. The term 'theme' denotes the theme of the whole work, and one cannot speak of the motif of a work, or even its recurrent motif.[40]

---

37. Millard J Erickson, *The Word Became Flesh: A Contemporary Incarnational Christology* (Grand Rapids: Baker Books, 1991), 42–44.
38. An anecdotal story by Irenaeus tells of Polycarp's story that John would not use a public bathhouse when he became aware that Cerinthus, 'the enemy of the truth' was present, *Adversus Haereses* Book III. 3.4.
39. Keener, *John,* 320, for example, seems to use the terms interchangeably, in speaking of Johannine christology. Considering it to be among the most exalted in the NT, he then proposes some other 'themes', such as 'the witness motif', and other 'themes of love, faith, life, and the world'.
40. David JA Clines, *The Theme of the Pentateuch,* JSOT, Supplement Series 10, edited by DJA Clines, PR Davies, DM Gunn (England: JSOT Press, 1982), 17–19.

It is suggested by John 20:30 that the fourth evangelist selected a number of miracles, which he called *signs* for his readers' consideration in order to stimulate belief in Jesus for salvation. The theme of John is introduced in the Prologue, where Jesus' divinity and humanity come together, 'the word became flesh'. His humanity was obvious for all to see, but his divinity had to be demonstrated in the divine person performing signs, a number of which pointed to his creative ability.

Changing water into wine required creative ability, even though some basic molecules were already present. His supernatural knowledge demonstrated in his conversation with the woman at the well indicates divinity. Multiplication of food obviously required creative work. Healing the lame man whose legs had not functioned for thirty-eight years necessitated changing atrophied muscles which very likely had turned to scar, into muscles with contracting cells and released joints. It was to highlight this amazing creative activity of the God-man that John mentioned the period of lameness. Healing the man born blind adds to the wonderment of this divine-human being. If the blind man had ever had any apparatus for seeing such as a retina and neural sensory system, it had never functioned and required creative ability to make him see for the first time. Climactically, resuscitating a dead man in whom putrefaction would undoubtedly have progressed after four days in a warm climate, required setting in motion countless body functions in an instant and by his word.

All this is reminiscent of the original creation which was wrought by the word of God. The mounting evidence indicating Jesus' ontology comes to a climax in the flow of blood and water from the side of the crucified, as a sign from his own body suggesting that he was both human and divine.

A question remains regarding the place of a large section of the Gospel in the farewell discourse, chapters 13–17, and how humanity and divinity may be detected in this. It is true that this section does not indicate divinity by miraculous signs on other people. I suggest that in this this section, more than anywhere else, the heart of the human and divine being is revealed. Here the heart of a human is seen seeking the welfare of his friends and not wanting to leave the bewildered group as orphans. At the same time, the heart of the divine man is seen desiring to return to the glory from which he came, a return which he knew would continue the redemptive process with the coming of the Spirit. Therefore, this section also fits in with the overarching theme.

The reason for rejecting the various suggested meanings for the flow of blood and water is because they do not mention the 'blood and water' *together*. Thus, the 'anti-docetic polemic' interpretation and the 'symbolism of the Spirit', as well as Haupt's idea of an entirely divine Jesus in John's Gospel fail to find an interpretation which mentions the two elements together. Although there are no other instances in the Gospels where blood and water are mentioned together, they are in 1 Jn 5:6 to explain how Jesus came into the world.

> Οὗτός ἐστιν ὁ ἐλθὼν δι' ὕδατος καὶ αἵματος, Ἰησοῦς Χριστός, οὐκ ἐν τῷ ὕδατι μόνον ἀλλ' ἐν τῷ ὕδατι καὶ ἐν τῷ αἵματι (This is the one who came by water and blood, Jesus Christ, not by water only but by water and by blood).

This is obviously an argument against docetic influences. It seems that at some time after the writing of the Gospel John was faced with the opposite error in the church, that of denying the humanity of Jesus. This declared that Jesus was entirely divine and only seemed to be human, hence Docetism. John's argument against this is seen at the outset of his first letter, 1 John 1:1.

> Ὃ ἦν ἀπ' ἀρχῆς, ὃ ἀκηκόαμεν, ὃ ἑωράκαμεν τοῖς ὀφθαλμοῖς ἡμῶν, ὃ ἐθεασάμεθα καὶ αἱ χεῖρες ἡμῶν ἐψηλάφησαν (The one who was from the beginning, whom we heard, whom we saw with our eyes, whom we looked upon and our hands felt)

Again in 4:2, 3 in his warning against false teaching he advises,

> πᾶν πνεῦμα ὃ ὁμολογεῖ Ἰησοῦν Χριστὸν ἐν σαρκὶ ἐληλυθότα ἐκ τοῦ θεοῦ ἐστιν, καὶ πᾶν πνεῦμα ὃ μὴ ὁμολογεῖ τὸν Ἰησοῦν (ἐν σαρκὶ ἐληλυθότα in many MSS) ἐκ τοῦ θεοῦ οὐκ ἔστιν
> (every spirit or teaching) which witnesses (teaches) that Jesus Christ has come in the flesh is from God and every spirit that witnesses or that does not teach that Jesus has come in the flesh is not from God)

Then he remembers again his analogical observation of the blood and water. The issue in 1 Jn 5:6 is how Jesus came. He came as the combination of deity and humanity, δι' ὕδατος καὶ αἵματος (by water and blood). The emphatic repetition, 'not by water only', is significant for anti-docetism. John understood that the humanity of Jesus was just as important as his divinity. The requirement of death for atonement could not be met by a totally divine being.

Smalley believes that the coming in water and blood means 'the terminal points of the earthly ministry of Jesus: his baptism at the beginning and his crucifixion at the end.'[41]

The reversal of the words water first and blood second is thought to be significant and they suit his interpretation, but it is not a strong argument. However, this kind of coming in Jesus' ministry ignores his original coming in divinity and humanity.

It may be concluded that a sympathetic witness watched the death of Jesus confirming that this man was really human. Later reflection regarding his Lord's humanity and divinity prompted John to consider the flow of blood and water as an appropriate analogy for expressing this truth. But *ichor* circulating in mythical gods was not real and neither were they. So John's conclusion was at best a metaphorical hint to Jesus' divinity. Surely he had witnessed further evidence of divinity in his teacher.

---

41. S Smalley, *1, 2, 3 John* in Word Biblical Commentary, General editor, DA Hubbard, Volume 51 (Waco, Texas: Word Books, 1984), 277–283.

Chapter Three
Evidence for the Divinity of Jesus

The concept of divinity is used here to mean the property of being God and that which pertains to God and to no one else. However, someone who originated directly from God's being and not by God's creativity may also be called divine. This excludes other heavenly beings such as angelic messengers who were created. It seems that the purpose of God was not to send to earth a super-human being with unearthly cosmic powers which cannot but demonstrate the presence of a god. Therefore, the divinity of Jesus was necessarily a cryptic and implied divinity. A being such as that which appeared to Saul of Tarsus in a glorified state in Acts 9 and claimed to be Jesus is too inhuman to be considered a human being. The divine-human redeemer had to be human among humans and had to imply his hidden divinity by various clues which might be understood after his work of atonement was accomplished.

Jesus implied his divinity from the multitude of his miraculous works, from his implied authority over the scriptures and the Sabbath, and from his claim to the sonship of God. It will be asserted that this was a unique and literal sonship, but could be perceived to be cryptically a metaphorical sonship similar to that of other Jews. Following his resurrection, those who saw him alive again and those who believed in him found it natural to believe in his divinity and to worship him. A number of ways in which Jesus' divinity was implied are discussed below.

Merciful Miracle Worker

First, Jesus implied his divinity by the things he did when he mercifully performed many miraculous works for people who were unwell physically, mentally and spiritually. He even calmed a storm threatening to sink a boat, fed thousands of hungry people by multiplying food and raised some people from death to their previous life. All of this prompted the observation from the crowds saying 'When the Messiah comes will he do more miraculous signs than this man?' (Jn 7:31), implying that this might be the Messiah. Similarly, Jesus himself confirmed their observation, 'If I had not done among them what no one else did, they would not be guilty of sin' (Jn 15:24). Although the Messiah may have been perceived by those expecting his coming to be entirely human, the multitude of miracles performed by Jesus appears to have been performed by his own volition and by his own power without appealing to the intervention of any other divine name. This is suggestive of his divine authority in utilizing divine power.

Jesus the Son of man

Second, among the many statements of Jesus reported in the Gospels, some implied his divinity. Jesus understood that he had originated from God as son of God as well as from a human, son of man. But he knew better than to make a clear claim to literal divine parentage in the ardently monotheistic culture in which he lived. Both of these self-designations as son of God and son of man were ambiguous. Son of man referred to being a human being as used many times in the language of Ezekiel, and son of God could be understood with a metaphorical meaning. It was used at the time, as James Dunn points out, for Israeli kings, for Prophets, for the expected Messiah, for angels and for individual Israelites.[1]

However, the 'son of man' self-designation was used almost exclusively by Jesus and was a harmless enough claim unless it was associated with the characteristics described by the prophecy in Daniel 7:9–10, 13–14. In Daniel's vision it is said that 'there came with the clouds of heaven one like a son of man, and was given to him dominion, and glory, and a kingdom, that all the peoples, nations, and languages should serve him'. Jesus' method of conveying this implication about himself was to include it in his sayings and allow

---

1. James DG Dunn, *Christology in the Making: A New Testament Inquiry into the Origins of the Doctrine of the Incarnation*, second edition (Grand Rapids MI: Eerdmans, 1989), 13–22.

the claim to dawn upon his disciples after his resurrection when he had achieved what he came to do. On reflection upon his statements and actions, his followers could come to the realization that he was indeed the divine son of man. Craig Evans identifies at least 16 uses of the term 'son of man' with this meaning mixed with a total of at least 80 uses of it in the Gospels.[2] It was conveniently cryptic and camouflaged Jesus' intention to identify himself with the prophetic glorified figure in Daniel.

Jesus implies his divinity by the authority and the prerogatives given to the son of man. With the prerogative to forgive sins, the son of man hints at undeniable divinity, since 'who but God can forgive sins?' (Mk 2:10, Lk 7:48). In his claim to lordship over the Jewish sacred day, the Sabbath, he affirms, 'therefore, the son of man is lord also of the Sabbath', among other lordships (Mk 2:28). The Sabbath was sanctified by God (Gen 2:2–3), and yet Jesus claims an authority second only to God's. But this authoritative son of man came to give his life a ransom for many (Mk 10:45) so that his mission on earth, the salvation of humankind, might be accomplished. As a result of the son of man's redemption of those who believe in him, the son of man's kingdom will be cleansed by his angels, so that his own people will shine as bright as the sun (Mt 13:41–43).

A number of 'son of man' designations refer to his return to earth in glory. As predicted in Daniel, Jesus claims that he, the son of man, will sit on the throne of his glory (Mt 19:28, Lk 22:28–30), and he will come with the clouds of heaven (Mk 13:26; 14:62, Mt 24:30). Readiness for the son of man's return is advised as it will happen unexpectedly (Mt 24:37, 39, 44). At one point, in John 12:32–34, he must have been talking of himself as the son of man, but claiming that if he were lifted up from the earth in crucifixion, he would draw all to himself. But they were taught that the Messiah lives for ever. So how could he talk of the son of man being lifted up? 'Who is this son of man' was an understandable question which was not answered plainly. But as the time for his being lifted up from the earth approached, Jesus claimed clearly to be that son of man. He affirmed, 'from now on you will see the son of man seated at the right of the power and coming on the

---

2. Craig Evans, 'The Self-Designation "The Son of Man" and the Recognition of His Divinity', in *The Trinity: An Interdisciplinary Symposium on the Trinity*, edited by Stephen T Davis, Daniel Kendall and G O'Collins (Oxford: University Press, 1999), 29–47.

clouds of heaven' (Mt 26: 64, Mk14:62). This clinched his guilt in the eyes of the Jewish leaders of making himself to be divine.

Authoritative Statements

Third, and in addition to the 'son of man' statements, Jesus also implied his divinity by a number of habitual ways in which he spoke in his teaching claiming unusual authority in what he said. He frequently prefaced his statement with 'Amen, I say to you' in many places in the synoptic Gospels, and the repeated 'Amen, amen I say to you' in John, rather than using the usual prophetic 'Thus says the Lord'. This implied that his statements had his own divine authority much like God's. Added to this, in his proclamations in the Sermon on the Mount in Matthew, he feels free to modify statements of the Mosaic Law with 'But I say to you', thus exercising an authority which would be thought to be God's alone. However, he could exercise such prerogatives as one who was in a close filial relationship with God. His claim to be the son of God is a major subject and will be discussed under his self-consciousness (chapter 5) where the literality of his genetic descent from God will be proposed.

Jesus Worshipped

Fourth, an activity which implies Jesus' divinity is the response of early believers who rendered worship to Jesus as to a deity. Such response relies on the intuitive perception of worshippers who believe that the person worshipped has exhibited evidence of divinity. In the case of Jesus, his miraculous activity and his resurrection were considered sufficient to ascribe divinity to him and so early believers' devotion is considered to constitute worship.

In his letter to the emperor Trajan, Pliny the Younger, in about 111-113 CE, as governor of Bithynia, wrote what he probably learned from some Christians. He says that they 'assemble before daylight' and that 'they recite by turns a form of words to Christ as god'.[3] A statement like this from an enemy of Christianity particularly lends support to the general perception that Jesus was worshipped.

---

3. Pliny, *Epistle* 10.96.

In modern times, the worship of Jesus is suggested in Larry Hurtado's note of six devotional practices which are detectable in the early church.[4] These are: Christ hymns sung to Jesus, prayer to God in Jesus' name and a few prayers spoken directly to Jesus, calling on Jesus' name as calling on a deity, partaking of a sacred meal, the Lord's table, in honour of a deity, confessing Jesus as Lord, and Christian prophecy as spoken by Jesus.

However, the worship of Jesus may not have been the same as the worship of God. The activity of worship at the time of Jesus seems to have had two nuances. One consisted of obeisance or bowing or even falling down on one's face as a gesture of deep respect. At times this was performed by one human being to another as well as to a deity. The other nuance of worship was confined to devotion to God. Jesus was offered the former kind of worship which seems to have been a gesture of respect during his pre-resurrection life.

Even though Peter refused the worship or obeisance from Cornelius in Acts 10: 26, and though the angel refused a similar action from John in Revelation 22:9, this kind of obeisance was reasonably common. It exhibited high esteem or reverence from one human to another as exemplified by the debtor making obeisance to the creditor in Matthew 18:26.

Two words are used for worship by Jesus in his encounter with Satan in his temptation in Matthew 4:10. At this encounter Satan desired from Jesus 'obeisance', a falling down before him, προσκύνησις, (worship) which acknowledges some kind of respect and even surrender to the one so worshipped. The other word used for worship was λατρεῖα, latreia (worship) which has the meaning to serve in a devotional manner. Jesus uses both for the worship of God in his reply. He says, Κύριον τὸν θεόν σου προσκυνήσεις καὶ αὐτῷ μόνῳ λατρεύσεις, (You shall bow down in worship [do obeisance] to the Lord your God and only to him shall you do devotional service).

This reference originates in Deuteronomy 6:13 and Exodus 20:5 where it is noted that the emphatic prohibitions μόνῳ, (only) and οὐδὲ μή (definitely not) accompany service, (λατρεῖα) alone. It is

---

4. Larry Hurtado, *One God, One Lord: Early Christian Devotion and Ancient Jewish Monotheism* (Minneapolis: Fortress Press, 1988), 100-114, and *How on Earth Did Jesus Become a God: Historical Questions about Earliest Devotion to Jesus* (Grand Rapids MI: Eerdmans, 2005), 28. Hurtado sees here an indication of binitarianism, but at least they indicate a perception of divinity

noted that 'latreia' λατρεῖα, (devotional service) is used only in the worship of God and never of Jesus, whereas obeisance is used for Jesus as well as other people. It may be deduced that Jesus, though divine, was a lesser deity than God the Father. Should Jesus be worshipped by rendering him 'latreia', (devotional service), particularly if one only God is to be so worshipped?

A study by James DG Dunn, *Did the first Christians worship Jesus? The New Testament evidence* (London: SPCK, 2010), 57 indicates some doubt that Jesus was worshipped by the first Christians. Dunn notes that Jesus was central to early Christian worship.

> He was the reason why their prayers could be offered with confidence and the principal subject of their hymns. It was his name they invoked; they appealed to him in times of personal crisis. And their praise of God naturally included praise of Christ ... It was his day on which they met regularly. Their sacred meal was his supper, the key elements his body and blood....

All this sounds as much like the rendering of 'devotional service, latreia', λατρεῖα, to Jesus as to the one God. If it is the case that this act of worship has changed from Old Testament costly sacrifices to heart-felt worship by mouth and in words of devotion, then it seems that such sacrifice is offered to Jesus as well as to God. The idea complies with Hurtado's suggestion and is expressed by Hebrews 13:15, as the way God is to be worshipped today, 'Through Jesus, therefore, let us continually offer to God a sacrifice of praise—the fruit of lips that confess his name'. But this is offered to God 'through' Jesus or because of that which Jesus had achieved, and if Jesus is offered the same, it indicates the worship of at least two deities.

Dunn claims that 'few prayers as such are recorded as being made to Jesus; few hymns are recorded as being sung to Jesus; no sacrifices were offered to him as to a god'. Therefore, should the question posed by the book ask 'whether Jesus had somehow replaced a remote God, so that worship is now to be directed to him, perhaps even to him rather than to God' (page 58 of the book). Dunn concludes (page 151) that worship

> should always be offered in the recognition that God is all in all, and the majesty of the Lord Jesus in the end of the day expresses and affirms the majesty of the one God more clearly than anything in the world.

The question as to whether or not Jesus should be worshipped and whether worship should be offered to one God or more than one depends on what is perceived to be the union between God and Jesus in his glorification. In such union it is questioned whether the mention of one deity's name in worship or prayer limits what is offered to the deity named. An attempt to provide an answer to this question is included in chapter seven, 'Implications for the Trinity' where it will be proposed that due to the present union between three divinities, worship of one named deity results in the worship of all three.

Paul's Perception of Jesus and God

Fifth, the evidence provided by Saul of Tarsus is significant and implies Jesus' divinity. Saul was a man who had a first-hand experience of meeting the risen and glorified Jesus who appeared to him on the way to Damascus in blinding light, resulting in his own blindness, and subsequently in his conversion (Acts 9). Some years later, as an established missionary, Paul would mention God and Jesus together in benedictions and prayers. In Paul's letters he implies that Jesus is divine like God. For example, he writes, 'Grace and peace from God our Father and the Lord Jesus Christ' at the beginning of a number of his letters (Rom 1:7, 1 Cor 1:3, 2 Cor1: 2, Gal 1:3-4, Phil 1:2, Phlm 3). At the end of his letters Paul prays for 'the grace of the Lord Jesus Christ' upon his churches (Rom 16:20b, 1 Cor 16:23, Gal 6:18, 1 Thess 5:28, Phlm 25. In 2 Cor 13:14 God and the Holy Spirit are added). This suggests that Paul thought of God and Jesus in very close proximity to one another, suggesting divinity for both. He felt free to write of Jesus, ὅτι ἐν αὐτῷ κατοικεῖ πᾶν τὸ πλήρωμα τῆς θεότητος σωματικῶς, (for in him dwells all the fullness of divinity bodily) (Col 2: 9), indicating that Jesus is in reality divine.

Jesus' Resurrection

The sixth category provides the most convincing evidence for Jesus' divinity, the evidence of his resurrection from death. From the descriptions provided, this was a unique event, entirely different from any resuscitation from death which had been performed by Jesus and others, in which dead people were revived to their previous way of life. The descriptions of Jesus' resurrection included the appearance and disappearance of his body at will, emphasised by 'the doors being locked' (Jn 20:26) and ultimately by his body being seen to be elevated to the sky in his ascension (Mk 16:19, Lk 24:51).

In his book, *The Resurrection of God Incarnate*[5] Richard Swinburne argues that a God incarnate would be expected to be raised from the dead and that Jesus' resurrection is evidence that he was God incarnate. Swinburne's argument begins with the existence of a God who is able to perform such a resurrection and that he had reason to do so. Evidence for the existence of God is provided in his *The Existence of God*.[6] The reason for the provision of a divine-human being is for the requirement of a sinless human life to be offered sacrificially to God to make atonement for human wrong-doing. An entirely human life was not available to meet this requirement and therefore a divine-human life was provided. Evidence that Jesus qualified for such a requirement is readily available from the records, and no one in human history had these qualifications.

Further, evidence for the satisfactory acceptance by God of Jesus' offering of his life and sacrifice, is indicated by his resurrection as God's endorsement of Jesus. It could be viewed as God's signature that a satisfactory transaction had been reached between God and people who would make this sacrifice their atoning offering to God.[7] The mathematical formula for calculating this kind of probability is found in Swinburne's writings.[8] The accomplishment of human atonement required Jesus' evident resurrection and the event supports the truth of it and God's motive for sending a divine Redeemer.

Jesus called 'God'

If the above categories of Jesus' implying his divinity provide reasonable evidence for it, and if such divinity was derived from the divinity of God, could he be regarded as being God? The revelation

---

5. *The Resurrection of God Incarnate* (Oxford: Clarendon Press, 2003).
6. *The Existence of God* (Oxford: Clarendon Press, first edition 1979, second (Oxford: Clarendon Press, 2004).
7. Swinburne, *The Resurrection of God Incarnate*, 37–47.
8. Also a useful explanation is Eliezer S Yudkowsky, 'An Intuitive Explanation of Bayes' Theorem <http://yudkowsky.net/rational/bayes>. A new version has been placed on line. Accessed on 9 January 2018.

to the Hebrews was that there was only one God in existence as in Deut 6: 4, 'Hear Israel, the Lord your God, the Lord is one'. If Jesus was the one God of Israel, then some kind of metamorphosis needs to be postulated by which God transformed himself into a human being. The idea is rejected as some form of Modalism in which one God is revealed at one time as the Father, at another time as the Son, and at another time as the Holy Spirit. This kind of metamorphosis is denied by Jesus by talking to people about God and by addressing God as another individual apart from himself. Others also referred to the relationship between two individuals as 'God and Father of our Lord Jesus Christ' (Eph 1:3, 17, 1 Pet 1:3, Rom 15:6, Jn 20:17).

Undoubtedly the Hebrew perception was that of monotheism. If, for the reasons listed above, Jesus was perceived to have an ontology that was beyond that of an ordinary human being because he performed divine actions, then he could be called 'God' with the meaning that he was divine. Care is required not to usurp the position and authority of the one and only God. Even though this nomination risked compromising monotheism, the risk was taken by Christians in order to express the belief that this person was so connected to God, that in his divinity he could be called 'God'. The connection was explained by Jesus himself as that of a close father-son relationship.

It is noted that Jesus himself never made the claim to be the one and only God, but others' proclamation could be perceived to be so. Thus, the Jews angrily understood such a claim, a disciple in a surprised outburst called him 'My Lord and my God', another disciple interpreted the name 'Emmanuel, God with us', as applicable to him, the writer to the Hebrews asserts that this Davidic king is God, and early believers suggested that he was 'God incarnate'. How these are to be interpreted is suggested below.

Jesus and the Jews

On two occasions in the Gospel of John Jesus was accused by Jewish leaders of making himself equal with God (5:18), and making himself to be God (10:33). On the former occasion Jesus had healed a chronically lame man on the Sabbath and he claimed that as his Father was free from criticism for working on the Sabbath, so he was also (v.17). The Jews fixed their attention on his ownership of God as his Father and accused him of making himself equal with God. They said, οὐ μόνον ἔλυεν τὸ σάββατον, ἀλλὰ καὶ πατέραν ἴδιον ἔλεγεν τὸν θεόν ἴσον ἑαυτὸν ποιῶν τῷ θεῷ. (Not only was he breaking the Sabbath, but he was calling God his own father, thus making himself equal with God),

It is interesting that to the Hebrew mind a literal sonship tended to identify in some way the son with the father.

On the second occasion Jesus claimed that he and the Father are one in the sense that they both seek the safety of believers in a relationship similar to that of sheep with their shepherd. He claimed that no one can snatch the sheep out of his hands, and as the Father is greater than Jesus, no one can snatch them out of the Father's hands, and so, in that sense, Jesus and the Father are one in protecting their sheep.

This, however, was understood to be blasphemy because σὺ ἄνθρωπος ὢν ποιεῖς σεαυτὸν θεόν (you, a man, claim to be God) (Jn 10:33). Jesus' answer is unusual in quoting Psalm 82:6,

Οὐκ ἔστιν γεγραμμένον ἐν τῷ νόμῳ ὑμῶν ὅτι 'Ἐγὼ εἶπα, θεοί ἐστε; (Is it not written in your Law, 'I have said you are gods?)

The original quotation in the Psalms continues with 'and all of you [are] children of the Highest', which suggests that the meaning of Jesus was about children of God who, because of their perceived filial relationship were called gods. The meaning was not that these metaphorical children were in reality gods, but it was to emphasise the importance of the relationship. The discussion continues with, 'Why then do you accuse me of blasphemy because I said, "I am God's son?"' meaning since you are God's sons too. The reality, however, was that Jesus understood his special relationship with God which differed substantially from theirs because he knew that he was in reality ontologically divine. At the same time, he was denying the accusation of making himself God the Father. Thus a son of God could be perceived to be divine.

Jesus and Thomas

Jesus' first post-resurrection meeting with Thomas records the reaction of a disciple who did not believe that Jesus was raised from the dead. He doubted the reports of his fellow-disciples and perhaps believed that they had seen a spirit rather than the resurrected body of their teacher. In John 20:28, faced with the physical evidence of Jesus standing before him and issuing the invitation, 'Put your finger here and see my hands and reach your hand and put it into my side, and stop disbelieving but believe', Thomas' outburst of surprise addressed to Jesus was ʽΟ κύριός μου καὶ ὁ θεός μου (My Lord and my God!) The fact that Jesus failed to correct the title 'God' is said to be an admission of acceptance that he was God.

Technically, there are different words for God, (θεός), and for divine, (θεῖος) in Greek. The idea of divinity is found in Acts 17:29 οὐ τὸ θεῖον εἶναι ὅμοιον, (the divine is not similar) to manufactured things, and in 2 Peter 1:3, 4, there is a divine power, (θείας δυνάμεος), and 'we may be partakers of the divine nature', (θείας φύσεως). The available different wording that John could have used for Thomas' probable Aramaic, such as 'my divine Lord', (ὁ θεῖος κύριός μου), would not have conveyed accurately Thomas' sudden emotional expression. Therefore, Thomas, in his emotional upheaval, probably uttered 'my Lord and my God' in his Aramaic dialect. Yet from his monotheistic background he would not have considered the risen Jesus to be the one and only God, but one who was as close to God as possible. The risk of expressing ditheism was not Thomas' concern at the time. Hence Thomas' meaning could be taken to mean that Jesus was divine.

That Thomas considered Jesus to be a theophany of God is unlikely since he had been shown the wounds inflicted at the crucifixion. The lack of correction by Jesus of any wrong theology indicates that the subject of the conversation was not whether or not Jesus was God, but belief in Jesus' resurrection and perhaps his divinity. This is indicated by Jesus' announcement that in the future those who believe without seeing as Thomas had seen will be blessed.

Emmanuel

The name 'Emmanuel' meaning 'God with us' is another instance in which Jesus is said to be called 'God'. Matthew hears the story of the virginal conception, perhaps from Luke (see the discussion on the testimony of Mary and Joseph chapter five), and is impressed by the desire of God to save his people. He hears that a virgin became pregnant from Holy Spirit (or from God-as-spirit, chapter 5, fn 16), and is to bear a son who is to be called Jesus, meaning 'Saviour' because he will save his people from their sins (Mt 1:21–23). This brings to mind a past prophecy of salvation by God.

Historically, Ahaz, king of Judah, was being threatened by Pekah, king of Israel and Rezin, king of Syria, because they wanted him to join them in a coalition against Assyria in c 735 BCE. However, Ahaz was determined to agree to terms of peace with Assyria, while the prophet Isaiah advised him to trust in God alone. As a sign that God would save him and Judah, the prophet gave Ahaz a predicted time-line. By the time a virgin, any virgin, becomes pregnant and bears a child and the child reaches a certain age, the threat will be removed. This will be recognized as the intervention of God, and will be remembered by calling such a child 'Emmanuel', meaning God [has been] with us (Isa 7:14).

It is unclear whether a child was born and was called by this name, or if the emphasis was on a predicted time-line for God's intervention. But Pekah and Rezin were assassinated in c. 732 BCE, about three years later. The only clue to anyone named Emmanuel seems to be in Isaiah 8:8, 10, where God gave another prophecy addressing Emmanuel as representative of the people of Judah, and warning of a disaster.

However, though the salvation of God prophesied in the name of the first child was to be wrought through the manipulation of armies, Matthew understood that the second child who was actually born of a virgin would bring the ontological presence of God by the birth of God's son to the world for the salvation of God's people. Hence this event matches the prophecy for 'Emmanuel, God with us'. This understanding by Matthew may be proposed because it is twice mentioned in the story that the child's conception would be ἐκ πνεύματος ἁγίου (from or out of spirit holy). Therefore, Matthew was not suggesting that God would transform himself into this baby, and yet this child would have an origin from God and be regarded as divine.

'Your Throne, O God'

The writer to the Hebrews wants to affirm that Jesus is greater and better than all the Old Testament persons and institutions. But he begins by claiming that Jesus is greater than the angels. He chooses to use parts of Psalm 45 which is addressed to a king and in enthusiastic hyperbole the Psalmist calls the king *God*, meaning divine, even though the king is obviously a human being. Quoting parts of the Psalm verbatim makes it difficult to know what the writer of Hebrews wants to emphasize. In the long list of quotations from the Old Testament, the writer uses the repetition λέγει, (he says), to claim that it is God who is making these announcements.

In Hebrews 1:8, Ὁ θρόνος σου ὁ θεὸς εἰς τὸν αἰῶνα τοῦ αἰῶνος (your throne, O God, will last for ever and ever). 'God' is correctly understood to be in the vocative case. That this means 'divine' rather than the metamorphosis of the one and only God is seen in the next verse in which he addresses the enthroned as, ἔχρισέν σε ὁ θεὸς ὁ θεός σου ἔλεον ἀγαλιάσεως, (the God, your God, has anointed you with the oil of joy), the addressee being anointed by God, his God. Although the same word is used for God three times, the context is clear that in verse eight it is used in the vocative, while in verse nine both uses are in the nominative case, the second accentuating the first. The conclusion is that the writer to the Hebrews wished to affirm the divinity of Jesus by calling him *God* and meaning *divine*, much the same as did Thomas.

God Incarnate

The title 'God Incarnate' was given to Jesus by ancient theologians as early as the Apostolic Fathers interpreting John 1:14 'the word became flesh'. Even before this, a poem or song of the early church is recited by Paul in I Tim 3:16, beginning with Ὅς ἐφανερώθη ἐν σαρκί, (Who appeared in the flesh). In spite of some later MSS suggesting that, Ὅς, (Who), in 'Who appeared in the flesh' is a reference to God, (Aland et al *The Greek New Testament* note 2 for 'Who' in verse 16), the rest of the poem is obviously referring to Jesus. Therefore, Ὅς, (Who), is also taken to refer to Jesus, a human being who was also divine. As noted above, the risk of compromising monotheism is taken in order to affirm the divinity of Jesus.

The Only-Begotten God

John's statement that 'the only-begotten God who was in the bosom of the Father' (Jn 1: 18) is discussed in chapter 4.

In each of the instances of calling Jesus 'God' a theophany or metamorphosis of God is rejected. Apart from the accusation by Jewish leaders that Jesus was making himself to be equal with God and making himself to be God, all the other instances in which Jesus was called 'God' were a way of declaring his divinity.

The wording of patristic theologians is often dramatized for emphasis. The Nicene theologians noted Jesus' origin, as mentioned in the introduction, and they continue their description of the divine offspring, as

> Θεὸν ἐκ Θεοῦ, Φῶς ἐκ Φωτός, Θεὸν ἀληθινὸν ἐκ Θεοῦ ἀληθινοῦ, γεννηθέντα, οὐ ποιηθέντα (lines 8-11), (God out of God, Light out of Light, real God out of real God, begotten, not created).

Obviously, the offspring is not the parent. But calling Jesus *God* has produced a dilemma in Christological thinking if the calling is taken at face value without seeking the reality behind it. There must be a reality which is designated by language described by analogy, metaphor and *synecdoche*. A resolution of this dilemma will be proposed by a methodology for the way in which Jesus' unique ontology had been achieved.

Chapter Four
A Methodology by Which Jesus Could Be Human and Divine

The methodology of Jesus' hereditary divinity and humanity is the main topic of this investigation. Since historical information about Jesus describes him as a human being born of a human mother, his conception is an appropriate starting point for a consideration of his ontology. For the possible methodologies to be discussed, some basic scientific understanding is presupposed and is briefly outlined below.

Humans and their DNA

Human beings are composed of a variety of tissues which are constituted of an estimated 65 trillion cells. Each cell's function is determined to a large extent by 46 chromosomes in each cell's nucleus. Chromosomes consist of very long molecules of DNA *Deoxyribonucleic acid*. Each molecule has a double helical structure which resembles a spiral ladder. The rungs of the ladder are formed from the base pairs, *adenine, guanine, cytosine and thymine,* with two base-pair molecules forming the inner ends of any given rung of the ladder. These rungs are held together by hydrogen bonds which may be easily broken to separate the two strands of the spiral ladder. *Adenine* always binds with *thymine,* a purine with a pyrimidine, as *cytosine* also binds with *guanine.*

The two strands of the DNA molecule are complementary in the siting of their bases. Just as a sequence of letters can carry a message that depends on the ordering of the letters, so metaphorically the sequence of bases on the rungs of the ladder carries a message written in the four letter alphabet consisting of the bases A, C, G, and T. A gene is a long string of these letters carrying the information for the manufacture of a protein, so that a gene is analogous to a programme for a particular protein. Proteins are composed of amino acids and each group of three nucleotides, a *codon*, codes for an amino acid. Thus there are 64 possible triplets available for coding the 20 amino acids.

The *genome* consists of a complete set of genes and is very large. The human genome is over 3.5 billion letters long, although that which is considered to be functioning DNA is only 3% in humans. The remaining 97% of the DNA is non-coding 'junk' DNA analogous to 'junk mail'. However, this is responsible for the regulation, maintenance and reprograming of the genetic process, disabling some genes and enabling the inactivity of other genes. It is used in forensic genetic fingerprinting. The importance of DNA in this investigation is that it is the molecule of heredity, containing the characteristics passed on from parents to offspring and it is proposed that this mechanism was in process in the ontology of Jesus as in other human beings.

In addition, human beings are often described as having personality or mind, soul or spirit. The origin of personality is debatable, whether it is directly and completely determined by the physical make-up of its body or that persons consist of more than may be deduced by their genetic makeup. Objective evidence is sought in the investigation into the inheritance of human behaviour and personal traits other than physical, from studies of identical twins. Physical resemblances are obvious in such tweens and extend often to the pitch of their voices and some mannerisms.

Studies in identical twins which have been separated at birth and adopted into different home environments allow the assessment of the inheritance of particular traits without the contribution of genetic influence. The contribution to particular personality traits by heredity is thought to be of the order of fifty per cent or less.[1] Therefore it is suggested that although heredity is important in many personality traits, in none of the behavioural traits studied is genetic influence entirely determinative as the factor involved in one's personality. The environment of the individual, both internally in the body and externally in society, plays a prominent role, as do the individual free will choices that one makes.[2] Concepts such as these are introduced here because, as a human being, Jesus' ontology would also have included such elements.

---

1. Francis S Collins, *The Language of God* (New York: Free Press, 2006), 258.
2. Collins, *The Language of God*, 263.

Human reproduction occurs by conception, pregnancy and birth. Conception begins by the entry of male genetic elements, *chromosomes* containing genes, into the female ovum which already contains corresponding elements, thus forming one cell. A human gamete contains 23 chromosomes, half the number contained in a somatic cell, and the union of male and female gametes completes the somatic cell number of 46 chromosomes. The new cell begins to divide by each chromosome splitting lengthwise and forming a corresponding new helical chromosomal strand using material from cellular substrate, that is, non-genetic substances. When division of the cell is complete, each new cell contains 46 chromosomes. The process is repeated many times, thus developing a new individual, the product of two parents.

In humans, fertilization of the ovum by the contents of a sperm takes place inside one of the uterine, *fallopian*, tubes as the ovum travels along the tube towards the uterus after ovulation. The resultant complete cell, the zygote, multiplies by cell division, and when the small multicellular embryonic mass reaches the uterus, it becomes implanted into the uterine mucosa. Here, a foetus grows and develops for the next nine months until birth, when a new individual emerges into the world. The characteristics of the new individual are determined to a considerable extent by the genes inherited from its two parents. Genes situated on corresponding locations on a pair of chromosomes, the 'alleles', may be dominant or recessive in their expression of characteristics. This simplified account of genetics is also described by Collins and John C Lenox.[3]

Jesus' Possible Ontologies

If it is the case that Jesus was really human, his body must have been composed of cells whose nuclei contained 46 chromosomes. Half of these would have been contributed by Mary at his conception. The question requiring resolution is the origin of the 23 male-like chromosomes required to fertilise the female ovum, whether their origin was human or divine. If they originated from a human male, then Jesus was ontologically entirely human, as in (H.1) an ordinary

---

3. Non-specialist descriptions of DNA are also provided by Collins, *The Language of God*, 102–105, and John C Lenox, *God's Undertaker* (Oxford: Lion Hudson plc, 2009), 135–147.

human being who was specially gifted by God, or (H.2) an ordinary human being who was somehow adopted by God and in the process was divinized, or (H.3) possibly derived from a specially created sperm. If the chromosomes originated from a deity, then Jesus was ontologically partly divine as in (D.1) by incarnation, or (D.2) by materialization of part of the spiritual substance of God into 23 chromosomes within an ovum produced by Mary.

A Humanistic Ontology

Jesus as an ordinary human being would be the biological son of Joseph and Mary of Nazareth and therefore entirely human in his physical genetic makeup, his 'genotype', as suggested by his apparent ontology, his 'phenotype'. As a result of Jesus' obvious human appearance and his human mode of dying, this view is possible if not for the provision of other information which suggests that he was also divine. Rejecting such information, some have held this humanistic view since the beginning of Christianity. But in modern times it re-emerged for public scrutiny in 1977 with the publication of *The Myth of God Incarnate* following a symposium by a gathering of English theologians.[4] On the premise that Christianity is constantly changing into forms that can be believable, it was felt that the time had come to put forward a more believable hypothesis concerning the doctrine of the incarnation, namely, that it did not occur literally, but was a metaphorical concept.

The view that the incarnation was mythical was thought to be widely held by contemporary theologians and it needed to be aired publicly. One motive for change may have been a vague miraculous Docetism that is implied by the incarnation of a pre-existent deity who appeared as a man but in reality was not. Frances Young observes,

> it is now accepted by the majority of Christian theologians that Jesus must have been an entirely normal human being, that any qualification of this implies some element of docetic thinking, and that docetism, however slight undermines the reality of the incarnation.[5]

---

4. John Hick, editor, *The Myth of God Incarnate*, first edition 1977, second edition 1993 (London: SCM Press, 1993), Preface to the 1977 edition.
5. Frances Young, 'Can there be any evidence?', in *Incarnation and Myth: The Debate Continued*, edited by Michael Goulder (London: SCM Press, 1979), 6.

But another motive may have been a perceived injustice if salvation is conditional on belief in a divine saviour who was not available to most of the people of the world because they have no opportunity to hear about him, believe, and be saved.[6]

This theory has much explanatory power and is the mechanism for the formation of every human being. However, apart from Jesus' own claims implying divinity and his authenticity for such claims endorsed by his resurrection, this theory lacks salvific effectiveness if reparation is required by God from humanity for the salvation of sinful human beings. If God's motive for Jesus' coming was not salvation by a divine-human substitute, it is difficult to explain the rationality and effectiveness of God's sacrificing one human being who is identical in all respects to all the others. The alternative to atonement for salvation is an exemplarist interpretation of the work of Christ. Against this, Charles FD Moule posits

> the 'soteriological test' of Christology – 'Can such a Christ be a Saviour?' The contributors to the Myth . . . their answer is that the Christ whom their position implies can be a Saviour and that he does show us that God is redemptively involved in the world's travail.

But the deficiency of the exemplarist notion of Jesus' work is that it leaves us 'without a gospel of the remaking of man'.[7]

This gospel of human remaking would necessitate atonement, but if human beings have done no wrong, or if God does not require reparation if they have, or if human beings have some other way of achieving reconciliation with God, then atonement is unnecessary.[8] John Hick, for example, does not see the necessity for the remaking of man, but sees a continuous process of man's continuing making. According to this view, the death of Jesus was an example, since as God incarnate he could not die. Hick seems to ascribe to Christians the belief that the totality of God was in Christ and if Christ dies, God dies. Therefore, he reasons that while a good human being can make the supreme sacrifice by giving his life for others, God cannot,

---

6. This is expressed by Hick in 'Jesus and the World Religions', *The Myth*, 167–185.
7. Charles FD Moule, 'Three Points', in *The Debate*, edited by Goulder, 139.
8. Maurice Wiles, 'Christianity without Incarnation?', in *The Myth*, edited by Hick, 9.

because God cannot cease to be God. Therefore, 'to speak literally of his [God's] death is to speak without meaning'.[9]

If redemption is unnecessary, the alternative theological hypothesis 'sees our present human existence as a phase in God's gradual creation of finite beings that are to live in conscious filial relationship to him'. This seems to be a long process which will transform human nature into one that God intends. 'Life as we know it is part of the continuing process of God's creative work'.[10] Therefore, the humanistic view sees Jesus to have been a good human being, but no more, and its rejection is justified because it is inadequate to explain what appears to be God's motive for the Jesus event.

Adoptionism

This is a variant of humanistic ontology in which the man Jesus composed of a human genotype inherited from Joseph and Mary was deified perhaps for the quality of his life in obedience to God. Any divinity ascribed to Jesus on the basis of such ontology would then be due to the entry into him of the metaphysical Spirit of God after his conception, at his baptism, or sometime during his earthly life. In this respect, Jesus would be ontologically no different from any prophet that God inspired to achieve his purposes. Thus adoptionism claims that Jesus became Son of God at a certain time in his life.

James Dunn suggests that early Christian perception of divinity rested on Jesus' resurrection as the time of his being appointed Son of God. The resurrection was therefore

> of central significance in determining his divine sonship, either as his installation to a status and prerogative not enjoyed before, or as a major enhancement of a sonship already enjoyed.[11]

This denies any thought of a pre-existent sonship. He also notices that Psalm 2:7 'You are my Son; today I have begotten you', which he believes was taken up by the first Christians as applying to Jesus, 'uses

---

9. John Hick, 'Incarnation and Atonement: Evil and Incarnation', in *The Debate*, edited by Goulder, 80.
10. Hick, *The Debate*, 80.
11. Dunn, *Christology*, 35.

the language of "begetting" and specifies a particular birthday, a day on which someone, the king, the Messiah, becomes God's Son". Thus,

> primitive Christian preaching seems to have regarded Jesus' resurrection as the day of his appointment to divine sonship, as the event by which he became God's son (Acts 13:33).

It has been suggested that the apostle Paul expressed an adoptionist view of Jesus in Romans 1:3-4 by claiming that Jesus was

> γενομένου ἐκ σπέρματος Δαυὶδ κατὰ σάρκα, (made of the seed of David according to the flesh), and that he was ὁρισθέντος υἱοῦ θεοῦ ἐν δυνάμει κατὰ πνεῦμα ἁγιωσύνης ἐξ ἀναστάσεως νεκρῶν, (appointed to be [declared to be] son of God in power according to the spirit of holiness by the resurrection of the dead).

This has been interpreted as the seed of David being appointed Son of God at the time of his resurrection.

However, the verb ὁρισθέντος has also been translated 'declared to be or shown to be in the sense of proved to be'.[12] But Dunn points out that there are no examples of the use of the verb with these meanings in the New Testament. In Luke 22: 22 Jesus speaks of 'his appointed destiny', Acts 2:23 speaks of 'the appointed purpose' of God, and Acts 17:31 speaks of 'the man whom he appointed'. Charles EB Cranfield agrees and points out that Acts 10:42, 11:29, 17: 26, 31 and Hebrews 4:7 similarly indicate 'appointed' as the meaning of ὁρίζειν.[13]

But this verb has at least two nuances. One is an appointment to a position or status which the appointee did not previously possess. The other is a clarification and a reminder of the object's status. As it applies to Jesus, the former meaning, that of a new appointment, is obviously adoptionist, while the latter, 'declared to be', emphasises the status which he already possessed.

All of the above-mentioned texts, except Acts 11:29 seem to refer to the fulfilment of a pre-determined status or plan of God

---

12. Both the NIV and the New Standard Version of the Bible translate it as 'declared to be'.
13. Charles EB Cranfield, *The Epistle to the Romans* in two volumes, The International Critical Commentary, General editors JA Emerton, CEB Cranfield, GN Stanton, Volume 1, (Edinburgh: T&T Clark, 1975), 61-64.

rather than to a new appointment, and therefore 'declared to be' seems to be the more correct translation. For example, Luke 22:22 speaks of the Son of Man κατὰ τὸ ὡρισμένον πορεύεται (going according to his pre-ordained destiny). Acts 2:23, refers to τοῦτον τῇ ὡρισμένῃ βουλῇ καὶ προγνώσει τοῦ θεοῦ (the pre-determined plan and foreknowledge of God). Acts 10:42 affirms that Jesus was, οὗτος ἐστιν ὁ ὡρισμένος ὑπὸ τοῦ θεοῦ κριτῆς ζώντων καὶ νεκρῶν (the one appointed by God as judge of the living and the dead). It is a possible suggestion that God thought of the idea of Jesus' appointment as judge after Jesus' resurrection and glorification. But God's foreknowledge and pre-planning makes this unlikely. It is more likely that God had this in mind when he planned redemption and pre-planning seems to be the natural way to understand these appointments.

Further, Acts 17:26, claims that long ago God ὁρίσας προστεταγμένους καιροὺς καὶ τὰς ὁροθεσίας τῆς κατοικίας αὐτῶν (had appointed pre-designated times and set boundaries where people should dwell). Acts 17:31 warns that 'God has set a day in which he will judge the world with justice by a man whom he has appointed, having given all proof by raising him from the dead'. God's plan to locate people and to exercise judgement and appoint a judge was not a new one that was thought of after Jesus' resurrection, but Jesus' rising was proof of his worthiness as the appointed judge. Hebrews 4:7 speaks of God's second offer for people to enter into his rest for salvation. Πάλιν τινὰ ὁρίζει ἡμέραν (Again he appointed a day). In one sense this is a new appointment compared with the old, but it was pre- planned by God for redemption. It may be seen that in the vast majority if instances the use of the verb ὁρίζειν (to appoint), must be taken with the foreknowledge of God in mind. The difference between Acts 11:29 and the others consists in fellow-believers planning for a current necessity to contribute against a famine and therefore is consistent with a new appointment.

John Chrysostom's doctrinal position is indicated in his translation of the word.[14]

---

14. John Chrysostom, Ἑρμηνεία εἰς τὴν πρὸς Ῥωμαίους ἐπιστολήν in *Patrologia Graeca*, edited by J-P Migne (Athenai: Kentron Paterikon Ekdoseon, 1987-), in 161 volumes, Volume 60, columns 391–682, column 397.

Τί οὖν ἐστιν˙Ορισθέντος; Δειχθέντος, ἀποφανθέντος, κριθέντος, ὁμολογηθέντος παρὰ τῆς ἁπάντων γνώμης καὶ ψήφου . . . (what then is 'appointed?' shown to be, declared to be, judged to be, confessed to be by everyone's opinion and vote).

As far as Paul's statement in Romans 1:3-4 is concerned, there is little doubt that ὁρισθέντος means 'declared to be' and Jesus' resurrection is stated as proof of his sonship from God.

The phrase κατὰ πνεῦμα ἁγιωσύνης, (according to the spirit of holiness) in Romans 1:4 most likely is a synonym for God-as-spirit who raises the dead. By this unique resurrection God vindicated this seed of David as the literal Son of God. The reason for 'literal' may be deduced from Psalm 2:7 if it is to be summoned as evidence for a time of appointment to sonship as understood by Dunn (above). The emphasis is not necessarily on σήμερον, (today), but rather on the two parallels, γεγέννηκα σε, (I have begotten you), and Υἱός μου εἶ σύ, (You are my son). The English translation 'I have become your father' in the NIV is too indefinite to express the action of giving birth or begetting and is misleadingly amenable to a son being adopted.

The verb γεννάν, (to give birth), is used for the contribution of both male and female parents to their offspring. It is used of the male parent many times in the genealogy described by Matthew. In this a father ἐγέννησεν (gave birth to), an offspring.[15] Thus, a translation in the case of the male parent would be to beget, to generate or to father his offspring. For the female parent the translation to give birth is readily understood. Therefore, the conclusion has to be that adoptionism is no advance on a purely humanistic ontology for Jesus.

A Specially Created Sperm

A specially created sperm fertilising a human ovum is another form of humanistic ontology. Older theories such as parthenogenesis or those currently understood as cloning have been discarded since the offspring would be female, the same as the mother with similar genes. However, the possibility that Jesus' genetic makeup consisted of 23 chromosomes from an ovum from Mary and 23 contributed

---

15. Matthew 1:1-17. In 39 uses of ἐγέννησεν the subject is male, he 'birthed' or begat.

by a specially created sperm with which God fertilised that ovum miraculously continues to be considered a possibility.[16] There is no reason why such a creature would be designated divine since it would have no origin from God's being, but would be created. One motive for proposing humanistic theories is possibly to avoid belief in the miraculous.

Incarnation

Incarnation is the commonest word used to refer to the coming of Jesus into the world. However, rather than describing a methodology by which the change from divinity to humanity took place, it seems to be an affirmation that a deity has turned itself into a human being. It differs from a brief theophany or an angelic manifestation in that the incarnate individual persists in the human state throughout life and exhibits a variety of what are thought to be divine characteristics. These do not necessarily display all that a divinity might possess and not necessarily all the time. The concept understands the spiritual deity to be the human individual in an arrangement designated Docetic because the individual 'seems to be' human but is thought to be really divine.

Incarnations had never been recorded in the Hebrew Scriptures inherited by the Christians, but were acceptable occurrences, with less obvious divine characteristics, in Greek mythology known to cultures into which Christianity had advanced. Here, the way incarnations were thought to be achieved was by the activity of a god in procreation, usually but not always, with a female human. Plutarch (c CE 47–120) explains this for the incarnation of Plato.[17] In these conversations, Tyndares the Spartan is said to affirm that pregnancy produced by a divinity may not be

> by a physical approach, like a man's, but by other kind of contact or touch, or by other agencies, that a god alters mortal nature and makes it pregnant with a more divine offspring . . .

---

16. Millard Erickson, *Christian Theology*, second edition (Grand Rapids: Baker Books, 1999), 769.
17. Plutarch, *Table Talk*, viii.1.2, *Plutarch's Complete Works Essays and Miscellanies* in three volumes, Volume III (New York: Thomas Y Crowell, 1909), 306–307.

Similarities to Jesus' incarnation cannot be missed, particularly as the god Apollo is supposed to have fathered Plato through his mother Amphictione, and her husband Ariston was prevented from having sexual intercourse with her until after the child's birth.[18] However, the timing of the story is unclear, and it could have been late enough to be a parody against Christianity. That early patristic thinkers were mindful of pagan incarnational stories is indicated by Origen (c 185–254) in his defence of the Christian belief in the incarnation of Jesus against the ridicule of Celsus. He asks why this incarnation is so strange when ancient Greeks had similar stories concerning Plato's incarnation.

Although it is tempting to suggest that Christians transferred mythical incarnational stories directly to Jesus' incarnation, Frances Young, in a thorough search into possible influences to the formulation of the Christian doctrine, finds it doubtful. In that investigation it is conceded that the doctrine of Jesus' incarnation did not arise out of reflection on biblical exposition of texts guided by the Holy Spirit as some may claim, but was influenced by the culture of the day.[19] However, Young does not identify any one of the ancient theories to be influential, and in fact questions theories which trace the origin of christological beliefs to the general Hellenistic religious and mythological environment.

> Each of the theories has been seriously questioned in detail, partly on grounds of sparsity or lateness of evidence, partly because none provides an exact analogy to Christian claims about Jesus. Yet ... it was the Greek-speaking Gentile converts who transformed Jesus, the Jewish Messiah of Palestine, into an incarnate divine being ... such a development was inconceivable, it is said, in the context of Jewish monotheism, only the syncretistic pagan environment can account for its origin.[20]

Young also points out that it is difficult at times to know how seriously the thinking people of the Hellenistic culture took the stories they told. Obviously the general population took them to be

---

18. Origen, PG, *Contra Celsum*, I. 37.
19. Young, 'A Cloud of Witnesses', in *Myth*, 23, 29.
20. Young, 'Two Roots', *Myth*, 98.

true (Acts 14:8–14). But others created stories as parodies to poke fun at Christian claims about Jesus once the Christian religion had advanced into Gentile territory.[21] It may be concluded that it was unlikely that Christian theologians directly transferred pagan myths to Christian incarnational belief.

Nevertheless, *logos* philosophy seems to have had great influence on *logos* theology, particularly as the term was rendered legitimate by its use in the prologue to the fourth Gospel. Theologians of the patristic age (c CE 100–451) commonly used the term *logos* in their christological discussions, and it was considered then, and continues to be today, that the *logos* appeared incarnate in the womb of Mary. Logically, to become incarnate the *logos* is assumed to have been a pre-existent deity. This idea had its derivation in philosophical claims concerning a deity but this had no christological connotations until Christians linked it with certain interpretations of the *logos* used by the fourth Evangelist. The difference between John's and mythological interpretations will be discussed later, but a suggested origin of the traditional doctrine of the incarnation from philosophical presuppositions is outlined below.

The philosopher Heraclitus of Ephesus (c.535–475 BCE), is credited as the first to use *logos* to mean 'reason'. Having abandoned ideas of poets and mythographers,[22] he introduced *reason* as being responsible for what exists. By mythographers he may have been deriding belief in some divine creator such as Zeus. He advises,

> οὐκ ἄν ἔτι πρέπον εἴη ποιηταῖς καὶ μυθογράφοις χρῆσθαι μάρτυσι περὶ τῶν ἀγνοουμένων . . . κατὰ τὸν Ἡράκλειτον. (it would no longer be proper to appeal to poets and mythographers to instruct us about unknown matters . . . as Heraclitus says)

He considered that there was an underlying *logos, reason, design*, in all that exists, and therefore, 'all things are one'. He recommends that

---

21. Young, 'Two Roots', in *Myth*, 90–91. Lucian regarded Christians gullible 'to revere exceptional prophets as gods'.
22. *Polybius* (c 200–218 BCE), 'The Histories', Loeb Classical Library, translated by WR Paton, edited by FW Walbank, C Habicht (Cambridge, Mass: Harvard University Press, 2011), in four volumes, volume ii, Book iv.

οὐκ ἐμοῦ ἀλλὰ τοῦ λόγου ἀκούσαντας ὁμολογεῖν σοφόν ἐστιν ἕν πάντα εἶναι.²³ (it wise to listen or pay attention to the logos rather than than to me for everything is one)

This oneness has been misinterpreted at times, but his most likely message is that all things, even opposites, have an explanation, *logos* (reason) for their existence, and therefore have, in a sense, an underlying unity.

Thereafter, philosophers could detect a *logos*, (reason or design) in the universe, and while some deduced from this the existence of a designer, others were satisfied with an impersonal reason for explaining the universe. Socrates (c 470-399 BCE) may have entertained an escape from mythical polytheism as well. It is interesting that at his famous trial, Plato's account of Socrates' *Apology*,' Ἀπολογία, (reply to charges), one of the charges was 'not acknowledging the gods that the city acknowledges', and another was corrupting the young of Athens with such ideas.²⁴ It may be that philosophical thought was tending towards a spiritual or metaphysical cause for the universe. Such teaching may have influenced Socrates' pupil, Plato.

Plato (c 429-347 BCE) does not use *logos* but a *World-Soul*, corresponding to *logos*, pervading the universe.²⁵ However, this entity was created by a Δημιουργός, (Creator), transliterated as *Demiurge* in many translations. Further, this Δημιουργός is said to be ἀγαθός, (good), in fact the embodiment of 'the Good', suggesting a personal Creator. In the dialogues recorded in the Πολιτεῖα, (The Republic), or (Citizenship), Plato hints at this Creator as a divine being who is so perfect that he is unchanging,

ἀδύνατον . . . καὶ θεῷ ἐθέλεν αὐτὸν ἀλλοιοῦν, ἀλλ᾽. . . κάλλιστος καὶ ἄριστος δυνατὸν ἕκαστος αὐτῶν μένει ἀεί ἁπλῶς ἐν αὑτοῦ μορφῇ.²⁶

---

23. GS Kirk, *Heraclitus: The Cosmic Fragments* (Cambridge: Cambridge University Press, 1954), 65.
24. *Plato*, 'Timaeus' LCL, translated by RG Bury (London: William Heinemann Ltd, 1929), 4, 7, 51.
25. *Plato*, LCL, Edited and translated by Chris Emly-Jones and William Preddy, (Cambridge, Massachusetts: Harvard University Press, 2017), 19a1ff, 24b8 and pages 91-94.
26. *Plato*, 'The Republic' in two volumes, XX, LCL, translated by P Shorely, edited by TE Page, E Capps (London: W. Heinemann, 1953), 188-193. Also, 'Timaeus', 8.

(it is impossible ... even for a god to wish to alter himself, but as it appears, each of them being the fairest and best, it is possible to abide for ever simply in his own form)

Any change, says Plato, would be a change for the worse

μεταβάλλει ἑαυτὸν ... ἐπὶ τὸ χεῖρον καὶ τὸ αἴσχιον
(changing himself [would be] for the worse and shameful).

This unchangeability in a deity becomes axiomatic and persists in later writers, including Christian theologians. However, the primary operation of the *Demiurge* was not to create the cosmos, but to construct the *World-Soul* who in turn performed the creation. Therefore, the transcendent deity required a less transcendent agent to relate to the material world. Thus for the first time an agent of God is proposed for the creation.

Aristotle (c 384–322 BCE) conceives of a world-wide force corresponding to the *logos* as the cause of creation. But in accordance with his philosophy of motion in which everything is moved by some mover, the highest entity is the Prime Mover who is ultimately responsible for motion and is unmoved by anything. He says, ἔστι τι ὃ οὐ κινούμενον κινεῖ (there is something which moves without being moved). Aristotle calls this originator of movement 'God' and also regards this deity to be unchangeable from its perfection,

δῆλον τοίνυν ὅτι τὸ θειότατον καὶ τιμιώτατον νοεῖ, καὶ οὐ μεταβάλλει. εἰς χεῖρον γὰρ ἡ μεταβολή, καὶ κίνησις τις ἤδη τὸ τοιοῦτον.
(that which is most divine and estimable, and does not change; for the change would be for the worse, and anything of this kind would immediately imply some sort of motion)

Aristotle adds that this divinity ἀλλὰ μὴν καὶ ὅτι ἀπαθὲς καὶ ἀναλλοίωτον (being unchangeable, is also impassible [without feeling]).[27] Since the prime mover is so transcendent and impassible, a secondary mover is implied as the one who relates to the creation and this is equivalent to the *logos*.

---

27. *Aristotle* LCL, in 23 Volumes, 'Metaphysics' Volume II, Book XII (L) translated by H Tredennick (London: W Heinemann, 1969), 1074b line 25, 165, 1073a, 151, 152

Stoicism founded by Zeno of Citium (c 300 BCE) with contribution by Chrysippus conceived of the *logos* as a material force which pervaded the formless matter of the universe and organized it into rational form, and if divine, the *logos* was some kind of panentheistic deity within the universe.

Revived or Middle Platonism followed by Albinus tended to be more theistic than Stoicism and accepted a hierarchy of divinities, the highest being the first or *Supreme Mind* which coincides with the Aristotelian Unmoveable Mover. Emanating from this is the *World Intellect* or *second Mind* which coincides with the *logos,* a purposeful intellect through which God, the first Mind, created the world since a God who is perfect and unchanging would not directly be involved with such activity.

In the context of such philosophical background arose Philo of Alexandria (c 30 BCE – c CE 45), a devout Jew of the diaspora, who also contributed to the idea of the *logos,* but as a monotheist, he could not envisage a series of intermediary divinities emanating from God to do God's will. Instead, he considered these emanations to be God's δυνάμεις, (powers) and as such, they represented the means by which God undertook various activities, such as the creation and the government of the universe.

> πατὴρ μὲν ὅλων ὁ μέσος . . . κυρίῳ ὀνόματι καλεῖται ὁ ὤν, αἱ δὲ παρ' ἑκάτερα αἱ πρεσβύταται καὶ ἐγγυτάτω τοῦ ὄντος δυνάμεις, ἡ μὲν ποιητική, ἡ δ' αὖ βασιλική,
> (the central place is held by the Father of the Universe . . . called He [the Being, a translation of YHWH in the LXX] as his proper name, while on either side of Him are the senior potencies, the nearest to Him, the creative and the regal).[28]

Yet he considered God to be utterly transcendent and unchanging as did previous philosophers and wrote on the *logos* on which his writing is somewhat ambiguous. On the one hand, he considers the *logos* to be the most significant of God's powers, the reason or purpose of God in creation and government of the universe, [29]

---

28. *Philo,* in Greek with English translation by FH Colson and GH Whitaker, in *Philo,* LCL, in ten volumes (Cambridge, Masss: Harvard University Press, 1960), 20, 21. Volume VI 'On Abraham', 121, 62, 63
29. *Philo,* Volume II 'On the Cherubim' 36, 39, 31.

> ὁ δίοπος καὶ κυβερνήτης τοῦ παντὸς λόγος θεῖος, (the divine *logos*, the ruler and steersman of all).

On the other hand, he considers the *logos* to be the highest divine emanation from God through which the transcendent God achieves his purposes.

At times the second possibility seems to be indicated in his writing, suggesting that each Old Testament theophany was really an appearance of the *logos*,

> Ἄγαρ . . . ὑπαντήσαντος ἀγγέλου, ὅς ἐστιν θεῖος λόγος,
> (Hagar . . . when she met the angel who is divine logos . . .) [30]

Similarly, the change of names of Abraham and Jacob by ὁ ἄτρεπτος θεός (the unchangeable God), was due to the appearance and the action of the *logos* in

> μετωνόμασεν . . . ἄγγελος ὑπηρέτης τοῦ θεοῦ λόγος,
> (he changed the name . . . by an angel, God's minister, the *logos*).[31]

This contradiction in Philo's writing may be explained by attributing to the *logos* the status of an archangel created by God,

> ὁ λόγος δὲ τοῦ θεοῦ ὑπεράνω παντός ἐστι τοῦ κόσμου καὶ πρεσβύτατος καὶ γενικώτατος τῶν ὅσα γέγονεν,
> (and the logos of God is above all the world, and is the eldest and most all-embracing of all created things).[32]

It is of interest that some Christians have reasoned that as Jesus was the *logos*, then it was the pre-existent Jesus who undertook the visitations referred to above.

Philo continued with the idea that God is unchanging and even wrote *Quod Deus immutabilis sit, That God is unchangeable*. The title is quoted frequently as an indication that this was Philo's main thesis in his book, but it seems to apply only to sections 20–32 of 183 sections. Nevertheless, in section 22 Philo questions [33]

---

30. *Philo*, Volume II 'On the Cherubim', 3, 10, 11.
31. *Philo*, Volume V 'On the Change of Names', 87, 184, 185.
32. *Philo*, Volume I 'Allegorical Interpretation', 175, pages. 418, 419.
33. *Philo*, Volume III 'On the Unchangeableness of God' LCL, 3–27.

τί γὰρ ἂν ἀσέβημα μεῖζον γένοιτο τοῦ ὑπολαμβάνειν τὸν ἄτρεπτον τρέπεσθαι; (For what greater impiety could there be than to suppose that the Unchangeable changes?)

An attribute of unchangeability in God's being is assumed from his steadfastness. Wayne Grudem records that 'God is unchangeable in his being, perfections, purposes, and promises'.[34]

Texts used to prove this are, Malachi 3:6, 'I the Lord do not change. So you, O descendants of Jacob are not destroyed', emphasizes God's faithful continuing mercy. James 1:7 'Every good and perfect gift is from above, coming down from the Father of heavenly lights, who does not change like shifting shadows', emphasizes his faithful provision. In two texts God affirms his ability to perform his purposes. In Isaiah 46:10 'I say: My purpose will stand, and I will do all that I please', and Numbers 23:19 'God is not a man, that he should lie, nor the son of man, that he should change his mind. Does he speak and then not act? Does he promise and not fulfil?'

In fact God can change his mind when circumstances change. In Ex 32:9-14 God had threatened destruction of the disobedient Israelites. But after Moses' intercession, he relented. 'Then the Lord relented and did not bring on his people the disaster he had threatened'. Similarly, in Isaiah 38:1-6, having predicted Hezekiah's death, God added fifteen years to his life. 'I have heard your prayer and your tears; I will add fifteen years to your life'. In Job 3:4, 10 God had threatened Nineveh with destruction. But after they repented, 'When God saw what they did and how they turned from their evil ways, he had compassion and did not bring upon them the destruction he had threatened'.

On at least two occasions God was 'grieved' over his actions. In Genesis 6:6 'The Lord was grieved that he had made man on the earth, and his heart was filled with pain', and in 1 Samuel 15:10, 11 'Then the word of the Lord came to Samuel: "I am grieved that I have made Saul king, because he has turned away from me and has not carried out my instructions"'. It is noted that the biblical texts cited in support of such an attribute describe God's steadfastness and faithfulness rather than unchangeability in God's being or substance. Therefore God could contribute from his being to his son's conception.

---

34. Wayne Grudem, *Systematic Theology: An Introduction to Biblical Doctrine* (Grand Rapids: Inter-Varsity Press, 1994), 156-165, quoting Louis Berkhof.

In their contemplation on Christology, the early Christian theologians give an interpretation of the *logos* oscillating between the two meanings of the term, *utterance* and *reason*. The writings classed as the Apostolic Fathers (c 70–135 CE) designate Jesus by the *logos* title. For example, Ignatius, bishop of Antioch (d107–108) continues the idea of Jesus' divine incarnation initiated by John's Gospel. He calls Jesus αὐτοῦ λόγος ἀπὸ σιγῆς προελθών (his [God's] word emerging from silence),[35] presumably meaning that from the silence of God Jesus comes in revelation of God (Heb 1:1). Jesus was τοῦ πατρὸς γνώμη (the Father's mind or thought),[36] and he was τὸ ἀψευδὲς στόμα, ἐν ᾧ ὁ πατὴρ ἐλάλησεν ἀληθῶς (the unerring mouth by which the Father has spoken truly).[37] As to Jesus' humanity and carnation, Ignatius even calls him God who was conceived in a human

> ὁ γὰρ θεὸς ἡμῶν Ἰσοῦς ὁ Χριστὸς ἐκυοφορήθη ὑπὸ Μαρίας κατ' οἰκονομίαν θεοῦ ἐκ σπέρματος μὲν Δαυίδ, πνεύματος δὲ ἁγίου, (for our God, Jesus the Christ, was conceived by Mary according to God's plan, both from the seed of David and of spirit holy).[38]

Ignatius probably considered 'spirit holy' to be God-as-spirit, as suggested by

> εἷς ἰατρός ἐστιν, σαρκικός τε καὶ πευματικός, γεννητὸς καὶ ἀγέννητος, ἐν σαρκὶ γενόμενος θεός, ἐν θανάτῳ ζωὴ ἀληθινή, καὶ ἐκ Μαρίας καὶ ἐκ θεοῦ, πρῶτον παθητὸς καὶ τότε ἀπαθής, Ἰησοῦς Χριστὸς ὁ κύριος ἡμῶν.
> (For there is one physician, both fleshly and spiritual, born and unborn, God become in flesh, true life in death, from both Mary and God, first subject to suffering and then beyond suffering, Jesus Christ our Lord)[39]

---

35. *gnatius,* Letter to the Magnesians, 8, 2, in *The Apostolic Fathers*, LCL, Edited and translated by Bart D Ehrman (Cambridge, Massachusetts: Harvard University Press, 2003)
36. *Ignatius,* Letter to the Ephesians, 3, 2.
37. *Ignatius,* Romans 8, 2.
38. *Ignatius,* Ephesians 18, 2.
39. *Ignatius,* Ephesians 7, 2.

There is no suggestion that an entity other than God and Mary were involved in Jesus' conception, and a methodology such as a sexual encounter is not contemplated. Therefore, the event is regarded as a vague incarnation, very much like John's the *logos* became flesh.

The *logos* designation for Jesus is continued by the Apologists (c CE130–180) who sought to provide explanations for their faith to counter criticism from unbelievers and to support the faith of believers. Rejecting Ignatius' idea of Jesus being fathered directly by God, Justin Martyr (c 110–165 CE) compromised monotheism and provided proof that the *logos* was a second divine individual, God and the *logos* being numerically distinct (καὶ ἀριθμῷ ἕτερον).[40] He even provided proof against Jewish monotheism in interpreting the theophanies of the Old Testament as the appearances of this *hypostasis*, *logos*, on various occasions as man and angel and fire as in the burning bush to Moses.[41]

Nevertheless, Justin wants to affirm that τὴν δύναμιν ταύτην γεγεννῆσθαι ἀπὸ τοῦ πατρός (this hypostatic power is born of the Father), but does not divide up the Father who remains the same, (ἀλλὰ ταὐτοῦ μένοντος).[42] He believed that this individual was begotten before creation, and perhaps for the purpose of creation

> ὅτι γεγεννῆσθαι ὑπὸ τοῦ πατρὸς τοῦτο τὸ γέννημα πρὸ πάντων ἁπλῶς τῶν κτισμάτων ὁ λόγος ἐδήλου, καὶ τὸ γεννώμενον τοῦ γεννῶντος ἀριθμῷ ἕτερόν ἐστι, (that this offspring was begotten by the Father plainly before all created things the logos was made clear; and that which is begotten is numerically distinct from that which begat).[43]

That this begotten *logos* was for the creation is expressed as

> Δευτέραν μὲν γὰρ χώραν τῷ παρὰ θεοῦ λόγῳ, ὃν κεχιάσθαι ἐν τῷ παντί.[44] (For he gives the second place to

---

40. Justin Martyr, *Dialogue with Trypho* 128, 4 in Martin Sandig, *Ivstini Philosophi et Martyris Opera*, Wiesbaden, Οὐχ ὡς τοῦ ἡλίου φῶς ὀνόματι μόνον ἀριθμεῖται, ἀλλὰ καὶ ἀριθμῷ ἕτερόν ἐστι, (is not numbered as different in name only like the light of the sun, but is indeed something numerically distinct).
41. Justin, *Dialogue* 128, 4.
42. Justin, *Dialogue*, 128, 15.
43. Justin, *Dialogue*, 129, 9.
44. Justin, *Apology I*, 60, 9.

the *logos* which is with God, who, he said was placed crosswise in the universe),

Furthermore, Justin makes reference for this idea to Plato,

> Καὶ τὸ ἐν τῷ Πλάτωνι φυσιολογούμεν περὶ τοῦ υἱοῦ τοῦ θεοῦ, ὅτε λέγει, Ἐχίασεν αὐτὸν ἐν τῷ παντί, (And the physiological discussion concerning the Son of God in the Timaeus of Plato, where he says, 'He placed him crosswise') [in the form of a cross or X, suggesting the stamp of ownership upon the universe] [45]

This identifies God's Son and *logos* with Plato's *World-Soul* which produces a rational universe. Thus, the *logos* is not simply a power of God, but a second divinity, and Justin provides as evidence the use of the plural in the creation narrative, 'let us make man in our image' (Gen 1:26) showing that God was conversing with another who was presumably a rational being like himself.

In addition, the *logos* was God's wisdom (Prov 8:22 ff.), and the captain of God's hosts who appeared to Joshua.[46] The *logos*, having been put forth as an offspring from the Father, is divine, 'being Logos and first-begotten of God, He is God.'[47] However, this generation or emission does not entail any separation between the Father and the Son. This is an attempt by Justin to maintain a semblance of monotheism as is done by modern theologians.

Since the perceptions of the Apologists, Christology has not undergone great changes regarding the emergence of Jesus from God, other than Origen's idea that the *logos* was born in eternity or from the beginning ἀεὶ γεννᾷ αὐτόν, (he always or from the beginning gives him birth).[48] This is often called 'the eternal generation of the Son'. The word ἀεί can mean 'from the beginning' and the present tense of γεννᾷ (gives birth, begets) could be used as a historical present, as is used frequently in Greek. God having given birth at the beginning would be understandable, but God continually giving him birth would make no sense. Since the Son's deity is derived

---

45. Justin, *Apology I*, 60, 1.
46. Justin, *Dialogue*, 62, 2, 4.
47. Justin, *Apology I*, 63, 15; also *Dialogue*, 63, 5 and *Apology II*, 13, 4.
48. Origen, PG, *De Principiis*, I. 2, 4 'Because his generation is as eternal and everlasting as the brilliancy which is produced from the sun'.

from God, he may be called a second or secondary God, (δεύτερος θεός).⁴⁹ Later theological pronouncements have to do mainly with the relationship between the two natures of the Son, his human and his divine natures. Nevertheless, it is traditionally believed that it is this person, the *logos*, which became incarnate by some means, rather than God.

However, *logos* theology adopted properties and functions for God's *logos* similar to those understood by the philosophers. Thus, the *logos* was created or begotten, even at the beginning, for the purpose of compensating for God's transcendence for the creation of the universe, thus requiring an agent of creation. Since Jesus is perceived to be the *logos*, he is thought to have taken up some of these functions. Therefore, for the purpose of redemption, the *logos* is thought to have been a pre-existent deity who became human.

Although the problem of a transcendent God's relationship with the world seems to have been solved by the idea of *logos*, the relationship of the *logos* or second deity with God remains a problem. This then leads down complicated pre-historic trinitarian pathways which contribute to the complexity of Christianity. In response to this, the traditional incarnational doctrine has been called *mythical* as noted earlier, with Jesus considered to be genetically an ordinary man. This conclusion is unjustified without first considering other plausible means by which Jesus could have been divine as well as human. It is claimed that the methodology proposed in D2 provides such means using science and theology.

A Genetic Hereditary Methodology for the Divinity and Humanity of Jesus

A genetic hereditary methodology asserts that at a particular point in time, part of the immaterial, spiritual substance of God materialized into genetic material inside an ovum cell released from one of Mary's ovaries as the ovum travelled along the right or left uterine, *fallopian*, tube following a normal ovulation. The concept of God possessing substance is convincingly proposed by William P Alston.⁵⁰ It may be

---

49. Origen, *Contra Celsum*, V, 39.
50. William P Alston, 'Substance and the Trinity' in *The Trinity: An Interdisciplinary Symposium on the Trinity*, edited by Stephen T Davis, Daniel Kendal, Gerald O'Collins (Oxford: University Press, 1999), 179–201.

argued that God not being in the form of spiritual substance allows the idea that God could be an abstract thought in the human brain rather than an objective reality.

It is not possible to ascribe the measurement of size to a spirit, although greatness and power which are less specific categories may be ascribed to it. So the size of the creator God cannot be envisaged, even though God is understood to be omnipotent and very great, qualities which may be inferred from the size of the universe which he has created. Therefore, in considering that part of the spirit that is God which materialized, it may be inferred from biological analogy, that this *seed* of God was a relatively small part of God's spiritual substance, and certainly not the totality of God. Therefore, Jesus is not assumed to have been all that there is to God, but was the offspring of God. Statements by Jesus concerning his relationship with his Father, 'my Father is greater than I', (Jn14: 28 and others) are in keeping with this idea.

God's contribution to Jesus' genetic makeup was required to materialize from spirit in order to fertilise a material ovum contributed by Mary. The two contributions formed an embryo with a material human structure. It may be deduced that the genetic material from God was in the form of 23 chromosomes and equivalent to those contained in a male gamete. This divine contribution contained half the number of genes of a complete human cell. It is the number of chromosomes necessary to pair up with 23 chromosomes already in Mary's ovum.

It is the male gamete which contains a Y chromosome in the XY designation which is responsible for the male gender of the offspring. The female gamete contains two X chromosomes. Therefore, theoretically, half the offspring resulting from fertilization would be XX, female, and half would be XY, male. Jesus would have had in his cells XY chromosomes, and therefore the Y chromosome could be contributed only by a gamete with male characteristics. This denies the possibility of cloning.

Incarnation should be thought of as the materialisation of part of the spiritual substance of God rather than a metamorphosis of a pre-existent second deity in a tri-theistic company (my emphasis). Materialization within an ovum differs from any suggestion of a specially created sperm and natural fertilization, the penetration of a sperm through the wall of an ovum. This normally requires the presence of many sperm surrounding the ovum. In case this is linked to Hellenistic mythology in which gods were said to have inseminated women, it is emphasised that what is proposed here is an incarnation and materialisation of spiritual substance within an ovum cell and not an insemination of Mary by God.

The processes of genetic materialization, the pairing up of divinely-derived chromosomes with human chromosomes, and the commencement of division of the new cell explain only how the beginning of Jesus' life was both human and divine. Any continuing divinity for Jesus together with his humanity during his earthly life may be explained by the role played by the four chemical bases, *adenine, guanine, cytosine, and thymine* from each parent's DNA acting as templates for the formation of further DNA molecules at the time when cells divided. It is natural to envisage that Mary's DNA molecules would reproduce more DNA from the substrate, the circulating chemical substances, derived from her blood stream and her nutrition.

The question for the continuing divinity of Jesus is to consider what substrate is used by the divinely-derived DNA molecules to manufacture more divinely-derived DNA. The most likely origin of substrate from which further divinely-derived DNA is manufactured would also have come from Mary's blood stream and her nutrition. This would provide material substrate for the development of the zygote, embryo and infant until it could nourish itself. This is the same substrate used by Mary's DNA molecules to manufacture more humanly-derived DNA. The difference between the divinely-derived and humanly-derived DNA formed from the same substrate resides in the *pattern* of chemical bases. This pattern is the original pattern inherited from the divine father and another pattern is inherited from the human mother.

The reason why the same substrate may be used by paternal and maternal genes acting as templates is because it is the pattern of bases which is inherited by subsequent cells and not a continued inheritance of cellular and molecular material inherited originally from the parents. Therefore, even the divinely-derived chromosomes can copy their divine pattern using earthly, human molecules. The original molecules materialized from the divine spiritual substance are replicated many times at cell division, and after a number of divisions the actual cellular material contributed by God (and by

Mary) virtually disappears from the system of the offspring. This also happens in biological reproduction from two human parents. Nevertheless, the template or pattern exerts far reaching effects, as noted by the sometimes observed very close similarity of offspring to parents. This genetic similarity becomes evident in efforts to identify individuals by DNA analysis using the DNA of relatives.

It follows that the production of proteins from divinely-derived and humanly-derived templates could not be separated. They would have been incorporated together in Jesus' tissues and used in his metabolism. It may be theoretically postulated that some substances produced in Jesus' body might be somewhat different from those of other human beings as a result of being produced from divinely-derived patterns of nucleotides. Any divine origin ascribed to him would rely on the unique divine pattern of the arrangement of chemical bases in his DNA.

It was noted near the beginning of this chapter that as well as a physical component, human beings have a metaphysical or spiritual component. This seems to be very closely related to the physical. Support for this idea may be derived from a statement by Jesus who seemed to have an unusually profound understanding of human nature. In the absence of certain scientific evidence for such human component, Jesus' words are regarded insightful. He seemed to know about the existence of this part of human nature as well as the value of it. He said in Matthew 16:26,

> τί γὰρ ὠφεληθήσεται ἄνθρωπος ἐὰν τὸν κόσμον ὅλον κερδήσῃ τὴν δὲ ψυχὴν αὐτου ζημιωθῇ; ἢ τί δώσει ἄνθρωπος ἀντάλλαγμα τῆς ψυχῆς αὐτοῦ; (what shall it profit a human being if he or she should gain the whole world but lose their own soul? Or what shall a human give in exchange for their soul?)

As well as this human commodity, Jesus' spiritual origin from God-as-spirit would play a major role in his ontology. Thus a divine-human being came about, one which was qualitatively very different from ordinary human beings, as reported in some of his characteristics and activities and his perceived sinlessness.

The only alternative to the maintenance of Jesus' divinity would be a continuing materialisation from God's spiritual substance into the body of Jesus. However, this may be considered to be the operation of an unnecessary miracle on the part of God. Human parents pass on to their offspring some of their individual heritable characteristics, even though it is the pattern of nucleotides that is inherited. This pattern, in turn, makes use of earthly molecules repeatedly for the rest of the offspring's life. This could also be the case with Jesus, heredity being passed on from divine father and from human mother to the offspring, Jesus, constituting him as divine and human. Further, the phenomenon which is well known in genetics, of genes being dominant and recessive would also apply to Jesus. Thus, some divinely-derived genes acting as dominant genes, however they were formed, may have exerted an influence which would have been surprizing in an ordinary human being. His capabilities were also influenced by a strong spiritual closeness between Jesus and God which seemed to be a uniquely strong bond.

There remains a question regarding the suitability of Jesus' inheritance from Mary for the sinlessness of God's son. It is a universal observation that disobedience to God's expressed wishes constituting sin is found in the life and behaviour of every human being who is born of two human parents. Therefore, this propensity to sin must be passed on from parents to offspring in some way. It follows that the capability and even the propensity to sin would have been inherited by Mary from her parents and it would be reasonable to expect that this capability would have been passed on to her offspring, including Jesus.

However, the capability and even the propensity itself, does not seem to be sinful until it results in action as suggested by Jesus' regard for little children. He is reported in Mk 10:14 and Luke 18:16 as saying,

> "Ἀφετε τὰ παιδία ἔρχεσθαι πρός με, καὶ μὴ κωλύετε αὐτά, τῶν γὰρ τοιούτων ἐστὶν ἡ βασιλεία τοῦ θεοῦ
> (Allow the little children to come to me and do not hinder them, for of such is the kingdom of God).

Presumably the inheritance of such nature by little children does not in itself condemn them. Therefore, it may be assumed that Jesus inheritance of Mary's nature did not automatically cause him to sin, even though he was genuinely tempted. The reality of the temptations faced by Jesus is indicated by the writer to the Hebrews 4:15

> οὐ γὰρ ἔχομεν ἀρχιερέαν μὴ δυνάνενον συμπαθῆσαι ταῖς ἀσθενείαις ἡμῶν, πεπειρασμένον δὲ κατὰ πάντα καθ' ὁμοιότητα χωρὶς ἁμαρτίας (for we do not have a high priest who is unable to sympathize with our weaknesses, for he was tempted in all ways as we are yet without sin).

The question remains whether Mary's inherited fallen nature had any effect on Jesus' nature.

Human behaviour does not seem to depend entirely on one's genetic inheritance but is deemed to depend on choices for which humans are responsible.

In addition to what has been termed a fallen human nature inherited from his mother, Jesus also inherited a holy divine nature from his Father. These capabilities would not have been automatic influences, but depended on his choices, as suggested by his genuine temptations. Therefore, it may be concluded that Jesus inherited from his mother the capability to sin and the capability to die. He inherited from his Father the capability to be sinless and the capability to live eternally. He had the spiritual capability to choose. He chose to be sinless and he chose to die a human death.

The difference between Jesus and other human beings is that he was endowed with divine capabilities and a unique spiritual nature, whereas other human beings are not. This difference needs to be accepted even though it means that an entirely human being could not be offered to God for atonement for human sin. He was human enough to satisfy God's requirement for such reparation. Therefore, his faultless sacrifice satisfied God's demand for the divine-human substitute's payment for the sins of humanity. His resurrection as noted in chapter three indicated God's acceptance of his sacrifice and God's endorsement of his work.

Chapter Five
God's Literal Fatherhood of Jesus

Traditional theology understands Jesus' sonship from God the Father to be metaphorical rather than literal. If Jesus is claimed to be a second individual deity in eternity, there is hardly an alternative view than that of a non-literal sonship. However, the D.2 methodology as an explanation of Jesus' ontology requires God's literal fatherhood of Jesus. Evidence which is entirely scientific is not available to prove this proposition because there is no surviving DNA from Jesus to examine, and in any case, God being spirit, does not possess DNA in his being. Therefore, the main evidence available is that which indicates that God was Jesus' literal father from the biblical narrative. Apart from logical inference for this if no human male is implicated in his heredity, evidence is sought in the testimony of Mary and Joseph and in the examination of Jesus' filial relationship with God as it is reported in the Gospels.

Logical Inference from Genetics and God's Motive for Atonement

As Jesus' body was similar to those of other human beings, it was composed of cells with their required genetic code inherited from two parents. Therefore, Jesus must have had genetic heredity either from two human parents or one human and one divine, the divine contribution having become very similar to the human. A *docetic* presence in which a spiritual being appeared to be human but was not is not a logical contender of method. A divine heredity may be deduced because other methods of explanation for divinity in Jesus lack explanatory power. Adoptionism may be perceived to be an advance on an entirely human prophet in whom God-as-spirit resided, but God-as-spirit had come upon many human beings for inspiration and these were never perceived to be divine. The only other methodology, which is also hereditary, and which has adequate explanatory power is the humanistic explanation which views Jesus as the son of Joseph and Mary, but this lacks salvific effectiveness.

Apart from the denial by Mary and Joseph of a humanistic ontology, an entirely human being could not achieve salvation if atonement is required from sinful human beings. The relationship between God and humanity was damaged by human sin resulting in humans living unholy lives as is evident in human history. In such a relationship, it is up to the wronged person to determine what reparation is required from offenders to repair the relationship. It seems that the satisfaction of God's requirement was the offering of a sinless human life. Such life was impossible to find among humans. Therefore, God contributed divinity to the formation of the divine-human life of Jesus.[1] This motive seems to be the most logical reason why God would undergo an alteration in part of his spiritual substance in order to father an offspring with a human.

The Testimony of Mary and Joseph

The infancy narratives of Luke and Matthew, particularly the angelic announcements to Mary (Lk 1:26–38) and to Joseph in a dream (Mt 1:18–25), are the most supportive texts for a genetic divine ontology for Jesus. However, the historical reliability of the infancy narratives has been disputed. Evidence that the narratives are included in the ancient manuscripts is not lacking [2] yet their authorship and their origin from reliable sources are doubted by some.

Opinions regarding the authorship of the Gospels range from the view that none of the Gospels were authored by those whose names

---

1. Swinburne, *The Resurrection of God Incarnate*, 37--44.
2. The most ancient manuscript containing these narratives is p^4 (c.200), preserving parts of Luke 1-6, and p^{45} (c.200) contains substantial parts of the whole Gospel. The earliest complete copies of Luke appear in the uncial parchments of the fourth and fifth centuries. These are Codex Sainaticus, Alexandrinus, Vaticanus, and Ephraimi, James R Edwards, *The Gospel According to Luke* in the Pillar New Testament Commentary, General editor Donald A Carson (Grand Rapids: Eerdmans, 2015), 3, 4.

are appended to them ³ to the view that their titles include authorship at an early stage.⁴ As far as Luke is concerned, the external patristic evidence overwhelmingly favours the authorship of Luke for the Gospel and Acts.⁵ Against this is the perception that the theology of Paul in his letters does not match his theology described by Luke in Acts. Therefore, it is reasoned that Luke could not have been the author of Acts and the Gospel, which are allegedly the work of a later author. However, on the side of reliability is the opinion that subjective deduction from perceived internal evidence of theology is not as strong as the external historical evidence.

Authorship of the infancy narratives is important to indicate sources and their reliability. Commentators on the Gospels tend to focus on the sources of a whole Gospel and therefore posit the usual synoptic dependence of Luke and Matthew on Mark and Q, as well as the possibility of a Hebrew Gospel, and some edited information of the authors. Therefore, the sources of the infancy narratives are included with those of the whole Gospel which allegedly came from some ill-defined 'tradition' which may have circulated in the early Christian communities. Specialised works such as that of Raymond Brown's *Birth of the Messiah* are uncommon, although Brown also posits a 'tradition' source for the infancy narratives without any input from Jesus' family.⁶

Doubt regarding the reliability of these narratives is influenced also by their supernatural character which seems to some to be far from reality. Therefore, the passages have been given a variety of names including 'legend' which assumes its fictional genre.⁷ Darrell L Bock rightly suggests that

> one's judgement about historicity, especially in view of the presence of angels and a miraculous birth, depends more on

---

3. Brown, *Birth*, 27, allegedly the majority opinion.
4. Donald A Carson, Douglas J Moo, Leon Morris *An Introduction to the New Testament* (Leicester: Apollos, 1992), 66 cite Tertullian *Against Marcion*, 4.2 'a work ought not to be recognised . . . [unless it has] the fullness of the title and the just profession of its author'. Also, Martin Hengel, *Studies in the Gospel of Mark* (Philadelphia: Fortress, 1985), 64–84, claims that authorial additions were necessary before 100 CE.
5. Edwards, *Luke*, 5–8.
6. Brown, *The Birth*, 525, 526.
7. Darrell L Bock, *Luke* in two volumes, ECNT (Grand Rapids: Baker Books, 1994), 70.

how one sees God's activity in the world than on the data of the text ... though there is no doubt that the text's perspective sees the events as historical realities and calls the reader to see them in the same way.[8]

An historical source based on perceptions from the biblical account for Luke's information is not generally entertained other than by Burnett H Streeter and only in general terms. He acknowledges that Luke who had accompanied Paul when he was imprisoned in Caesarea, spent two years (Acts 24:27) in the region collecting information from eyewitnesses for his Luke-Acts.[9] Travelling to Jerusalem for this purpose was readily possible, as was obtaining information from Mary herself if she were still alive in CE 57–59. Luke's aim (Lk 1:1–4) and inquiring mind as a physician (Col 4:14), coupled with the confidence that his profession may have generated in Mary, may have allowed her to relate some personal details about the birth of Jesus which were unlikely to have been publicly circulated before this time.

Therefore, Luke's 'infancy narrative' and the story about the boy Jesus' visit to the temple in Lk 2:41–52 very likely had their origin from Mary in approximately CE 57–59.[10] The probability that Mary was still alive at this time is high. If Mary was aged fourteen or so at the time of the angelic announcement and conception of Jesus,[11] and if she gave birth at fifteen years of age, and if Herod died in 4 BCE which seems

---

8. Bock, *Luke*, 72.
9. Burnett H Streeter, *The Four Gospels: A Study of Origins* (London: Macmillan, first edition, 1924, second edition, 1953), 218. There an opportunity for Luke to make trips to Jerusalem from Caesarea to talk to those who were ἀπ' ἀρχῆς αὐτόπται, (from the beginning eyewitnesses), Luke 1:2. Among those consulted could have been Mary (if she were still alive and living in John's house as indicated in John 19:26–27).
10. Frederick F Bruce, *Paul: Apostle of the Heart Set Free* (Grand Rapids: Eerdmans, 1977), 475. Also, RT France alludes to the possibility that Luke may have had access to information that could ultimately come only from Mary, whether personally or not, 'Jesus Christ, Life and teaching of' in *The Illustrated Bible Dictionary edited by* JD Douglas, Frederick F Bruce, Randolph VG Tasker, James I Packer, Alan Millard (London: Inter- Varsity Press, 1998, 1962), 762.
11. The betrothal of girls in early teenage years is suggested in two articles by Craig S Keener, 'Marriage', 680, and 'Women in Greco-Roman World and Judaism', 1276–1280 in *Dictionary of New Testament Background* edited by Craig A Evans and Stanley E Porter (Downers Grove, Illinois: Inter Varsity Press, 2000).

to be the best reasoned view, then Jesus' birth would have occurred sometime before this, perhaps between 6 and 4 BCE. Therefore, at the turn of the millennium Mary would have been around twenty years of age. At the time of Luke's interviews in Jerusalem around CE 57–59, she would have been in her very late seventies or may be very early eighties. It is considered quite possible, then, that Mary was alive and was the source of Luke's information. Matthew's narrative could have been obtained from Luke by communication between the two authors.

The introduction in Luke 1:26–30 sets the scene, including Mary's surprise and anxiety at the appearance of an angel. The full content of the announcement vv 31–33 is overlooked by Mary except the first part, ἰδοὺ συλλήμψῃ ἐν γαστρί, (look! listen! you will become pregnant). Her question, 'How can this happen, since I do not know a man?' (in a sexual relationship) has generated some discussion, since as a young woman who was betrothed, in the normal course of events she would get married and soon after would probably become pregnant. Her natural perception would be expected to be that this announcement referred to a future time after she was married. Therefore, the announcement seems out of place, unless it was to affirm the high status of her offspring, and even then the announcement seems somewhat premature.

It is suggested that somehow Mary understood the announcement to be referring to an imminent pregnancy, even before marriage, which justifies her question.[12] It may be that Luke's inclusion of the introductory ἰδού inferred more than a casual commencement of a conversation with (Look!), but rather suggested immediacy and something out of the ordinary. Mary was very likely aware of other miraculous conceptions such as those of Abraham and Sarah, Elkanah and Hanna (1Sam 1:2–2:21), and currently Zechariah and Elizabeth, which involved a male and female. But what was implied by this announcement was unique, there being no male in a sexual relationship with her. Therefore, 'How can this be?' was a logical question.

The angelic response provided sufficient explanation to answer it,

---

12. Various reasons for the question are listed by Bock, *Luke*, 118-121, but the most likely reason for the question is Mary's understanding of an immediate conception.

Πνεῦμα ἅγιον ἐπελεύσεται ἐπὶ σὲ καὶ δύναμις ὑψίστου ἐπισκιάσει σοι. Διὸ καὶ τὸ γεννώμενον ἅγιον κληθήσεται υἱὸς θεοῦ. (Spirit holy will come upon you and the power of the Most High will overshadow you. Therefore, the one born will holy, and called the son of God).

Bock rejects any sexual connotation in this statement saying, 'The verb ἐπελεύσεται, will come upon, should not be over-pressed as a sexual allusion, since God can create life without a sexual act'.[13] Raymond E Brown agrees,[14] but David Daube sees sexual connotations in the use of the Semitic term 'to cover over or to spread (something) over a woman as a euphemism for sexual intercourse'.[15] The latter may be overstating the case for the verb to overshadow, but Mary did ask a sexual question in using 'knowing' as a common euphemism for sexual intercourse. The angelic reply to such a question was therefore thought likely to have sexual connotations.

Although the verb ἔρχομαι, (I come), in its various derivatives as in Exodus 19:15 μὴ προσέλθητε γυναικί, (do not come at a woman sexually)', and Leah to Jacob, Genesis 30:16, πρὸς ἐμὲ εἰσελεύσῃ σήμερον, (you must come to me today), implying a sexual act, it is also used of God coming upon people to inspire them. Thus, ἐγένετο, ἥλθατο, ἐφήλατο, ἐγενήθη, ἐπ'αὐτῷ πνεῦμα Θεοῦ, (there came upon him the spirit of God) (Num 24:2; 1Sam 10:10; 11:6; 19:23), describing inspiration of a human being.

The methodology proposed would side with Bock in rejecting a sexual connotation in this instance. The course to the ovum released from Mary's ovary would entail God-as-spirit entering Mary's abdomen akin to a surgical procedure. Detecting which of her two uterine tubes contained the ovum that month, part of the spiritual substance of God would enter the tube and the ovum and materialize there into 23 chromosomes. These would pair up with 23 chromosomes already in Mary's ovum to form a material zygote.

---

13. Bock, *Luke*, 121.
14. Raymond E Brown, *The Birth of the Messiah: A Commentary on the Infancy Narratives in Matthew and Luke* (London: Chapman/Gordon City, NY: Doubleday, 1977), 290. Commenting on Daube's claim, Brown claims that 'Though the Semitic term may be so used, ἐπισκιάζω never carries that connotation'
15. David Daube, *The New Testament and Rabbinic Judaism*. Jordan Lectures 1952, (London: University of London/Athlene 1956), 27, 32–36.

This would grow into an embryo which would be implanted into the uterine wall until birth. Therefore, it is unlikely that a sexual connotation is meant by the message from God through the angel. This unique miracle would indeed be an incarnation of some of the spiritual substance of God in an ovum.

Beginning with 'therefore' to justify the result, the difference between what had occurred in previous divinely-enabled conceptions and this unique one would be that God would be the literal father of the child. In biological fertilisation the addition of chromosomes to an ovum occurs from outside the ovum by the penetration of a sperm. However, what is suggested for the conception of Jesus is that part of the spirit that is God materialised within the ovum cell.

The concept of the Spirit of God in the Old Testament being identified with God-as-spirit instead of the Holy Spirit of Pentecost pointed out by James Dunn and Geoffrey Lampe is an important principle.[16] It is exemplified by parallelisms commonly observed in Old Testament writings. A couplet is noted in Genesis 1:1–2 where 'In the beginning God created the heavens and the earth, and [the] spirit of God was coming upon the water', both indicating that God-as-spirit was creating. Significant for the present discussion, another couplet is noted in the angelic announcement in Luke 1:35. In saying 'Spirit holy will come upon you, and the power of the Most High will overshadow you' the announcement referred to the activity of God-as-spirit in this conception, without implicating the third person of the Trinity.

Although other sonships of God found in Scripture are metaphorical, and have the broad meaning described by Dunn, that of kings, Israel, or even the human Messiah,[17] the sonship perceived by Mary and Joseph was undoubtedly a literal one. Luke's inclusion

---

16. Dunn, *Christology*, 133. Dunn rightly points out that pneuma agion (πνεῦμα ἅγιον), or 'Spirit of God' 'denotes the *effective divine power* ... in other words, on this understanding, *Spirit of God is in no sense distinct from God,* but is simply the power of God, *God himself acting powerfully in nature and upon men*' and there was no perception of a separate pre-existent hypostasis at this point. Although Dunn is talking about the idea of the spirit of God acting in the OT, this activity of God can certainly be applied to Luke 1:35. Also, Geoffrey WH Lampe, *God As Spirit: The Bampton Lectures,* 1976 (Oxford: Clarendon Press, 1977), especially 206–228.
17. Dunn, *Christology*, 13, 18.

of the visit of the boy Jesus to the temple, and of his understanding of God being his father rather than Joseph emphasizes Luke's understanding of God's literal fatherhood of Jesus, however vague the means of achieving that fatherhood may have been at the time. Scholarly opinion is similar for Matthew's as for Luke's infancy narrative as regards authorship and sources.

It is concluded that both stories of the experience of Mary and of Joseph, probably originated from Mary's testimony to Luke. Communication between Mary and Joseph of their experiences would be natural at the time of the events so that Mary was aware of Joseph's dream. Therefore, the testimony of Mary and Joseph seems to provide feasible evidence for God's literal fatherhood of Jesus.

Jesus' Self-Consciousness of God as His Literal Father

The self-consciousness of Jesus seems to be a taboo area of theological consideration because it is generally thought to be impossible to verify it by evidence. John AT Robinson claims, it

> has become a sort of 'no go area' for New Testament theology. It has been sealed off as a minefield into which none but fools would dare to venture.[18]

Indeed, since most of this evidence is found in the fourth Gospel, it is considered by many scholars that John's evidence is not credible and that Johannine texts cannot be legitimately used to convey Jesus' self-consciousness. It is claimed that these texts consist, not of Jesus' statements, but of made-up theology written by authors later than John. Perhaps the only legitimate connection with John is that it may have been written by one of John's followers who had received teaching from him over time. As a result, statements put into the mouth of Jesus were allegedly for the purpose of substantiating theology understood by others rather than statements uttered by Jesus himself and heard by John.

However, this is not a universal opinion. Frank Weston presents the traditional view that

---

18. John AT Robinson, *The Priority of John,* edited by J (*Chip*) F Coakley (London: SCM Press, 1985), 352.

> the most important evidence to the divine nature of Christ is that . . . [it is] based upon the revelation of His self-consciousness, His knowledge of His pre-existence, and His memory of the state of eternal glory [19]

The swing from this position, Robinson claims, has not been replaced by any credible theory.

> what lay at the centre of Jesus' life has been left blank, and indeed [it has been] regarded as forbidden territory. We can say what the church said about him, but we cannot say—or apparently be allowed to care what he thought about himself. He could have meant something entirely different . . . But what if he did not understand himself as anything like what the church proclaimed him to be?[20]

While it seems valid to judge the fourth Gospel as having a theological interpretation about Jesus, it is feasible to see this theological development as the statement of John's theological theme running through the Gospel, set in a historical narrative, and designed to convince readers that Jesus is worthy of their trust for salvation (Jn 20:31). As suggested previously in chapter two, the author of the Gospel had a theme in mind, an affirmation of the divinity and humanity of Jesus. The selection of 'signs' and discussions in support of his overarching theme does not necessarily mean that they are fictitious. The historical genre in which the theme is set suggests the likelihood that the author was in fact an eyewitness, particularly in the Jerusalem ministry of the historical Jesus.

Craig Blomberg correctly seeks to examine the historical reliability of the Gospel in many individual events rather than relying on a few selected ones which may not be representative. Thus his 'study of introductory and background considerations, as well as detailed examination of every passage, in order to assess historicity' provides evidence for the reliability of the Gospel.[21] Therefore, the investigation into Jesus' self-consciousness of God as his literal father is made with considerable confidence.

---

19. Frank Weston, *The One Christ: an enquiry into the manner of the incarnation* (London: Longmans, 1914), 38.
20. Robinson, *Priority*, 353.
21. Blomberg, *Historical Reliability of John*, 22–67.

Literal fatherhood, in contrast to adoptive or metaphorical fatherhood, demands some kind of physical ontological heredity passed on to the body of the offspring, usually by means of substance derived from the father's seed. But in order to assess Jesus' self-consciousness of God as his literal Father all the uses of the term 'father' are traced in the Gospels in various conversations. Statistical analysis of the use of the title 'father' has been carried out by Larry Hurtado[22] and before him by Joachim Jeremias.[23] The current investigation seeks to distinguish those statements which may refer to literal fatherhood from those in which the sense is of a metaphorical or adoptive fatherhood.

The use of the possessive pronoun by Jesus to qualify 'father' probably means literal fatherhood. An example in which the possessive pronoun qualifying 'father' is taken literally appears in Jn 5:17 where Jesus uses the pronoun μου, (my), to refer to God as his father. In the next verse, the Jews understood him to be referring to God as his own literal father, πατέρα ἴδιον ἔλεγεν τὸν θεόν, (he was calling God his own father). The Jews took particular note of the pronoun and interpreted literality in his statement, as noted in chapter three, under 'Jesus Called "God"'. A similar instance is noted in John 10:33. There are also references in which a strongly relational fatherhood is used by Jesus or on behalf of Jesus, where its use refers to intimacy between father and son.

Therefore, all the references to 'father' in the Gospels are examined and are divided into three groups. Unlike the statistical investigations already mentioned, the aim here is to identify not only the number of occurrences of the word, but to assess the meaning of these uses according to three categories. Thus, the general uses of 'father' are designated 'at arm's length' uses (A). These are almost synonymous with 'God', or 'Creator', and are often referred to as ὁ πατήρ (the Father). In some of these, the word 'father' is not even mentioned, but an equivalent, ὁ πέμψας or τοῦ πέμψαντος, (the sending one)

---

22. Larry W Hurtado, 'God' in *DJG*, Edited by JB Green, S McKnight, I Howard Marshall, (Leicester: InterVarsity Press, 1992), 270-282. Also DR Bauer, 'Son of God', in *DJG*, 769-775.
23. Joachim Jeremias, *The Prayers of Jesus*, (S.B.T. 6; London: SCM Press, 1967), 29-35.4.

is used with the same at arm's length meaning.[24] These instances are included with the general use since on seven occasions the participle is found to qualify the noun πατήρ, (father) (Jn 5:23, 37, 6: 44, 8:16, 12:49, 14: 24). Therefore, in the five instances in which the participle stands alone (Jn 5:30, 6:38, 6:39, 8:26, 8:29), it is considered that πατήρ, (father), is understood.

The second group, which are designated 'possessive' (B) are those in which the possessive pronoun is used with 'father', such as μου, τοῦ, αὐτοῦ, (my, his, of him), indicating Jesus.[25] Possessive pronouns are used also to indicate other people, such as σου, ὑμῶν, ἡμῶν, (you, your, our), and these are included in the general 'at arm's length' category because they do not apply to Jesus.

The third group, designated 'intimate' fatherhood (C)[26] include those instances in which *abba*, the Aramaic address to a father is used or even when the actual word is not used but thought to be appropriate because of direct address. Other instances counted in this category are those in which close unity is perceived such as Jesus and the Father being *in* one another, being one, seeing God, knowing one another, and God being Jesus' own father. The degree of interpretation inherent in this methodology is deemed to be acceptable in order to obtain a more accurate idea of the sense of what is being said by Jesus and others about this relationship.

Comparing the Synoptics' and John's different categories, the Synoptics have A 27, B 18, C 4, while John has A 77, B 23, C 22. In all, the Synoptics have 49, while John has 122. The classifications in the three categories in the four Gospels are: A 104, B 23, and C 26.

---

24. Matt 5:6, 45, 48, 6:1, 4, 6, 8, 9 (//Lk 11:2), 14 (// Mk 11:25), 15, 18 x2, 26, 32, // (Lk12: 30), 7:11 //(Lk 11:13), 10:20, 29//(Lk 12:6), 32B //(Lk12:8), 33B //(Lk12:9, 11:25 //(Lk10:21), 26 //(Lk10:21), 27BAA // (Lk10:22 BAA), 12:50B // (Mk3:35 A //Lk8:21), 13:43, 18:14, 23:9, 24:36 // (Mk 13:22), 25:34B //(Mk3:35, // Lk 8:21), 28:19. Lk unparalleled 12:32 A's in Jn 1:14, 18, 3:35, 4:21, 23, 5:19, 20, 21, 22, 23x2, 26, 30, 36x2, 37, 43, 45, 6:27, 37, 38, 39, 44, 45, 46x2, 57x2, 65, 8:16, 18, 26, 27, 28, 29, 38, 41, 42, 10:15x2, 29, 32, 36, 12:26, 49, 50, 13:1, 3, 14:6, 8, 9, 12, 16, 24, 26, 28x2, 31x2, 15:9, 16, 26x2, 16:3, 10, 17, 23, 25, 26, 27, 28x2, 32, 18:11, 17x2.
25. Matt 7:21, 10:32// (Lk12:8 A), 33// (Lk12:9 A), 11:27//(Lk10:22 B), 12:50, 15:13, 16:17, 27// (Mk 8:38 B), 18:10, 19, 35, 20:23, 25:34, 26:29, 53, Luke unparalleled: 2:49, 22:29, 24:49, Jn 2:16, 5:17, 5:43, 6:32, 8:19, 49, 54, 10:18, 25, 29, 37, 14:2, 21, 23, 15: 8, 10, 15, 23, 15:24, 20:17.
26. Matt26:39// (Mk.14:36 C // (Luke 22:42 C), 26:42 // (Mk 14:39 C). Luke unparalleled: 23:29, 46, Jn 5:18, 10:30, 38 (2X), 41, 12:27, 28, 14:7, 9, 10 (3X), 11 (2X), 13, 16:15, 17:1, 5, 11, 21, 24, 25.

All instances of the possessive pronoun with 'father' could have been used by a literal or a metaphorical son. However, the unusual knowledge demonstrated by Jesus at other times, coupled with his knowledge of his origin and purpose of his coming to the world, a literal meaning for 'my father' may be implied. It is of interest to note the very large number of times Jesus refers to God by fatherhood even in the 'at arm's length' category, some seventy-four times, when the word 'God' could have been used.

In the case of the 'intimate' uses, C, most of them in John, of being one with the Father, being in one another with the Father (10:30, 38, 14:11, 20), knowing the Father (17:25), of direct address to a father (11:41, 12:27, 28, 17:1, 5, 11, 24, 25) are more likely to be used by a literal son than a metaphorical one.

It is concluded with a reasonable degree of confidence that in these references Jesus did indeed have a consciousness of God as his literal father. The dilemma facing Jesus was how to express this during his pre-resurrection state and to whom he could mention such a challenging claim. To the Jews he could hint at it in a guarded fashion. But he felt greater freedom and confidence to speak plainly with his disciples about his intimate relationship with his Father. Hence most instances in the intimate category, C, (15 of 22 in John) are found in the privacy of the farewell discourse of the fourth Gospel.

The emphasis on fatherhood with a relative neglect of motherhood in one's ancestry stems from a perception from the science of the day that the life of the offspring depended on the seed of the father and the womb was something like an incubator to provide nourishment for the embryo until its birth. When such an idea originated is unclear, but it was known in Greek mythology. In Aeschylus's *The Eumenides* the god Apollo claims that the mother is only a *wet-nurse* and not the progenitor of a child, whose blood derives from its unique parent, the father.[27] Whether or not a similar legend was known to the Hebrews is unclear, but the statement that a woman's womb had been closed, often assumed by God, may suggest that she was unable to produce children due to a closure of the womb to the seed of the father, thereby preventing the beginning of embryonic life. In a male-dominated society generation or siring was the father's prerogative and fatherhood was of great importance in one's ancestry.

---

27. Aeschylus, *The Eumenides* translated by AJ Podlecki, (Warminster: Aris & Phillips, 1989), lines 657–661.

Therefore, at times a man was spoken of as being in the *loins* of his father before he was born and as such he took part in the actions of his father (Heb 7:4–10). However, the literality of such understanding is viewed with some suspicion by the author of Hebrews who adds, ὡς ἔπος εἰπεῖν, (so to speak). Today this may be suggested by the figure of speech of *synecdoche*[28] in which one's heredity is situated in one's parents and not one's whole being. It is concluded that there was in Jesus' mind a literal father-son relationship between himself and God.

---

28. Synecdoche means 'simultaneous understanding' and is a figure of speech in which a part of an object is nominated for the whole (such as 'all hands on deck') and vice versa ('the car has a puncture' when only the tyre is involved).

Chapter Six
Objections to the Hypothesis of Divinity by a Genetic Methodology: The Pre-existence of Jesus

Of the various hypotheses examined for the ontology of Jesus the humanistic and the adoptionist ontologies obviously object to his having any form of pre-existence as they are based on the assumption that an entirely human Jesus was born of two human parents. The former ontology sees Jesus remaining entirely human and being an example for other humans, while the latter sees him as a divinised human being however the possibility of this may be imagined. But the incarnational theory objects to a genetically-derived divinity on the grounds of a pre-existent Son of God. Logically, Jesus as a human being could not have pre-existed. But just as logically, if Jesus had divinity as well as humanity in his ontology, then his divinity from God must have pre-existed in some form since God is eternal.

Therefore, two possible forms of pre-existence for Jesus may be proposed. The simplest is the one detailed in scenario D2 in chapter 4 in which part of the one and only God contributed to Jesus from God's spiritual substance. The second form of pre-existence, influenced to some extent by Greek philosophy as suggested under the discussion on the Incarnation ch.3, claims that a second divine individual of an eternally trinitarian God somehow became incarnate to produce the earthly Son.

The concept of God existing as a Trinity eternally is so ingrained in theological thinking, that other evidence is ignored. For example, Charles H Dodd interprets John 16:28 containing the preposition ἐκ, (out of), as in ἐξῆλθον ἐκ τοῦ πατρὸς καὶ ἐλήλυθα εἰς τὸν κόσμον as (I issued out of the Father and came into the world).[1] This

---

1. Charles H Dodd, *The Interpretation of the Fourth Gospel* (Cambridge: University Press, 1954), 259. Dodd accepts the use of ἐκ in some less well attested manuscripts, whereas the best attested ones use παρά (from).

'issuing forth' denotes extraction or origin and is distinguished from παρά and ἀπό (from beside and separation from) respectively. So he claims that Jesus emerged out of God, that he is ἐκ τοῦ θεοῦ. In this sense, applicable to no prophet or messenger, Jesus is Son of God.

Nevertheless, in spite of what appears to Dodd to be obvious, that Jesus came out of God in some way, his theological presuppositions prevent him from reaching the next logical conclusion that God directly contributed to Jesus' ontology from his own substance. Rather he claims,

> The evangelist does not mean that the man Jesus of Nazareth had a divine parentage . . . Nor does John betray any knowledge or interest in the doctrine of the virgin birth of Christ, as it meets us in the First and Third Gospels and in Ignatius. In any case, it is evident that it is not by reason of a miraculous conception that he is designated Son of God, for that would mean that he began to be Son of God at birth; but this is emphatically not the evangelist's view. Christ existed on the heavenly plane before he appeared on earth, and was already the 'beloved Son' of God.[2]

Dodd provides as evidence for the last statement John 17:5 and 24 which are discussed below. Therefore, since the presupposition of Jesus' individual pre-existence is considered to be a given, any other possibility is rejected. To check this view, evidence for Jesus' pre-existence is sought in christological texts, including the body of the fourth Gospel, the prologue of John, Phil 2:6-11, and texts suggesting that Jesus was the agent of creation and therefore he must have pre-existed.

The Gospel of John

The Gospel of John is the only source of texts in which Jesus is said to have claimed pre-existence. Within the body of the Gospel, excluding the prologue to be discussed separately, there are seventeen references alluding to pre-existence. The Synoptic Gospels have no instances in which unmistakeable pre-existence could be understood.

---

2. Dodd, *The Interpretation*, 260. The mention of Ignatius is because, as one of the Apostolic Fathers, Ignatius is certain of the virgin birth, as noted under incarnation.

There is no suggestion of pre-existence in fifty-three references to sonship recorded in Matthew. A review of the other Synoptic Gospels similarly fails to indicate any pre-existence of the Son. References in John are 3:13, 31–32; 6:33, 38, 46, 51, 58, 62; 8:23, 42, 58; 13:3; 16:28, 17:5, 8, 24, 25. Traditionally, all seventeen statements are claimed to be referring to a *hypostatic* or individual pre-existence and that Jesus remembered on earth what he had experienced in heaven and in eternity.

However, no details are provided to describe heavenly pre-existent situations. The recurring affirmation is about belief that Jesus originated from God and came to earth to provide salvation to people whom God loves. The texts are distributed in various conversations expressing Jesus' statements.

1. In his conversation with the Pharisee Nicodemus (3:1–21) he informs this teacher of the Jews that the kingdom of God can be entered only by belief in ὁ ἐκ τοῦ οὐρανοῦ καταβάς (the one who came down from heaven) v 13. The conversation was about the means of entering the kingdom of God through the one who has come and by the revelation of the spirit of God.
2. The Baptist's conversation with his followers was about Jesus who is more than an earthly being but is ὁ ἄνωθεν ἐρχόμενος ἐπάνω πάντων ἐστίν (the one who comes from above is above all) 3:22–36. His work takes precedence over all.
3. Jesus' conversation with Jews after they had been fed with miraculously multiplied food from a mere handful (6:22–71), centers around the one who comes from above to give eternal life. He is similar, but superior to the manna which God sent to sustain the Israelites in the wilderness. The word καταβαίνω, (I come down), in its various forms is repeated three times, and again, the conversation is about salvation for those who trust him.
4. In conversations with Jews who were self-satisfied with their status as children of Abraham and as children of God, he informs them that their behavior reveals more about them than any historical status (8:21–59). God who controls history is the one who sent him to liberate them from their sin and their slavery to it (v 34), and the resultant death that it brings (v 51). Reference to Abraham seems to be the only text which suggests an individual pre-existence. The listeners are informed in 8:56–59, that Abraham ἠγαλλιάσατο ἵνα ἴδῃ τὴν ἡμέραν τὴν ἐμήν, καὶ εἶδεν

καὶ ἐχάρη (rejoiced greatly to see my day, and he saw it and was glad). As Abraham was not also pre-existent, the meaning refers to Abraham's belief in the blessing that God would provide for his descendants. However, πρὶν᾽ Ἀβραὰμ γενέσθαι ἐγὼ εἰμί (before Abraham came into being I am) (historical present for *was*) conveys some form of pre-existence (to be discussed below).

5. In private conversations with his followers, knowing that the time had come to leave this world and proceed to the Father, he washed his disciples' feet as a sign of his cleansing of them. In 16:28 he reminds them, ἐξῆλθον παρὰ (ἐκ) τοῦ πατρὸς καὶ ἐλήλυθα εἰς τὸν κόσμον· πάλιν ἀφίημι τὸν κόσμον καὶ πορεύομαι πρὸς τὸν πατέρα (I have emerged from (out of) the Father and have come into the world; again I leave the world and proceed to the Father).

6. In Jesus' conversation with his Father (17:5–25) he is anticipating his return to the glory which he experienced while in God, and all the while he is remembering the ones he had won for eternity. He repeats their belief that (v8) ἔγνωσαν ἀληθῶς ὅτι παρὰ σοῦ ἐξῆλθον, καὶ ἐπίστευσαν ὅτι σύ με ἀπέστειλας (they really understood that I emerged from you, and they believed that you sent me).

The obvious question is whether Jesus could have spoken like this if he were not an individual deity in heaven with God and remembered being there. A conclusion to some kind of pre-existence cannot be avoided even though the emphasis of Jesus was not so much on his heavenly situation, but on his coming from God and on the purpose for his coming.

One explanation for self-consciousness of being in God may be that every part of the spirit that is God experiences self-consciousness, unlike ordinary human beings in whom self-consciousness is located in the brain. Then, in his separate state as a divine-human being on earth, he could have remembered this experience and expressed it by using the figure of speech of *synecdoche*. By this means, he spoke of his total self as being in God when only the contribution of God to his conception was in God. Thus, Jesus experienced the glory of deity (17:5, 24) because he was part of that deity. Similarly he could say that he saw God (6:46) and knew God (17:25) because he was part of God. Existing before Abraham (8:58) was naturally part of this pre-emergent state in the substance of God. His being sent and coming down for the purpose of God for the redemption of humanity was something that he understood partly by his genetic capability and partly by his spiritual connection with his Father. It is concluded that in reality Jesus surely had a pre-existence, but probably one that was part of the spirit that is God and not necessarily as a separate individual deity.

Assuming that these statements of Jesus are accurately reported, his motive for making claims to this experience is intended to inform his hearers of the importance of God's intention for salvation. As a byproduct of this he also makes a claim to his divinity and the authority which that entails. At the same time he avoids usurping the authority of his Father. Since he could not use a scientific methodology to explain his origin from God and thereby claim divine authority for his statements, he used a cultural explanation, namely the authority of a son exercising the authority of a father.

The Prologue of John

The prologue of John serves as an introduction to the Gospel and is considered by some to have been written by a previous author and was adopted by the Gospel-writer as an appropriate introduction for his own presentation of Jesus.[3] A more convincing view is that of Donald Carson who believes that the Prologue was also written by the author of the Gospel. He lists parallels between the prologue and the rest of the book and claims that 'the rest of the book is nothing other than an expansion of this theme'.[4] Further 'the tightness of the connections between the Prologue and the Gospel render unlikely the view that the Prologue was composed by someone other than the Evangelist'.[5] Nevertheless, Carson accepts the likelihood that the prologue could have been written as an introduction after the completion of the rest of the Gospel and looked back on it as happens in many works.

This Prologue is often regarded as the reference par excellence for proving Jesus' pre-existence as an individual in heaven because he was the agent of creation. The assumption that John wanted to present Jesus as having emerged from God like God's word emerged

---

3. Dunn, *Christology*, 239–245 [30.1]
4. Carson, *The Gospel According to John*, 111.
5. Carson, *The Gospel According to John*, 111–112.

from God's mouth seems reasonable. But the assumption that Jesus was somehow an individual pre-existent deity called Word does not. Further, this deity, according to one interpretation of verse three, was God's agent of creation. Later this deity took on flesh and became incarnate as Jesus, and hence became known theologically as the incarnate Word.

This series of assumptions is reminiscent of the philosophical thinking about *logos* traced in the fourth chapter under the subheading D1 *Incarnation*. It was noted there that the philosophical belief of Plato and others was that a transcendent God could not relate creatively to the material universe. This necessitated the creation of a second deity which was less transcendent and could be God's agent of creation. Since the creation was observed to display some kind of design, the second deity was called *logos*, meaning (reason) from which the idea of design may be derived.

Liddell and Scott's lexicon insightfully describes the uses of the term λόγος as *the word by which the inward thought is expressed*, or it can mean *the inward thought itself* [6] (my emphasis). Hence its meaning is generally summarised as 'word' or 'reason'. This definition can therefore extend the meaning of *logos* to *word, utterance, language and talk*, as well as *thought, reason, intention* and *purpose*. Because the English translation of λόγος is generally confined to 'word' without any other possibility, in order to encompass the double Greek nuance, the transliterated term *logos* is used here instead of 'word' to refer to one or other meaning.

Rather than assuming that John followed the philosophical idea of *logos*, I suggest that he derived his idea from the perception of second generation Christians who considered the way in which God had revealed himself to the world. This is expressed in Hebrews 1:1 which asserts than God in times past and in various ways λαλήσας, (having spoken), to the Hebrew fathers in the prophets, in these last days ἐλάλησεν ἡμῖν (has spoken to us) in a son. In both cases, in the past and in the current days, the methods of revelation are designated God's speech, or revelation, the *logos* of God.

---

6. Henry Stuart Liddell and Robert Scott, *An Intermediate Greek-English Lexicon* founded upon the Seventh Edition of their Lexicon, (Oxford: Oxford University Press, 2000), 476–477.

If the above suggestion is correct, the interpretation of the first three verses of the Prologue take on a different nuance from the traditional. In contrast to the usual perception, this interpretation begins with one God in eternity without a second deity called *logos*, (Word). The first two verses speaking of λόγος, *logos* have in mind the internal meaning to say that the thought and intention of God was always to reveal himself to humankind. This intended *logos* was in and with God and could be called 'divine' (θεὸς ἦν ὁ λόγος, (God [divine] was the *logos*). That the term 'God' has on a few occasions been used to mean 'divine' is discussed in chapter three under the subheading 'Jesus called God'. Thus John's assertion begins with

> Ἐν ἀρχῇ ἦν ὁ λόγος, καὶ ὁ λόγος ἦν πρὸς τὸν θεόν, καὶ θεὸς ἦν ὁ λόγος, (In the beginning was the *logos* [intention, purpose], and the *logos* was with God, and God [divine] was the *logos*)

Again, it is emphasised that this was God's idea in

> οὗτος [ὁ λόγος] ἦν ἐν ἀρχῇ πρὸς τὸν θεόν (This [the *logos*, the revelatory intention] was at the beginning with God).

In verse three the term *logos* is understood by its pronoun and it is affirmed that an internal intention of God is expressed with the external meaning of *logos*, 'utterance' to create the universe. The beginning of the 'prophetic' means of revelation announces how the creation was brought about. Here the term *logos* coincides with the oft-repeated καὶ εἶπεν ὁ θεός, (and God said) in the creation narrative. Thus,

> πάντα δι' αὐτοῦ ἐγένετο καὶ χωρὶς αὐτοῦ [τοῦ λόγου τοῦ θεοῦ] ἐγένετο οὐδὲ ἕν or οὐδέν. (all things were made through it and without it [the logos, word of God] nothing was made).[7]

---

7. A stop after οὐδὲ ἕν. is noted in the Aland *et al* editors of the fourth revised edition UBS *The Greek New Testament* (Stuttgart: Deutsche, 1994), also followed by the NRSV, but not the NIV.

Then John hones in on God's revelation in a son at the end of v 3 and beginning of v 4 to say that the divine intention, God's *logos* gave rise to, or resulted in, a life, a human life.

> ὃ γέγονεν ἐν αὐτῷ [τῷ λόγῳ] ζωὴ ἦν, (what happened to it [the logos, intention of God] was that it became [resulted in] life)

This was the life of Jesus and the purpose of this life was that it should be a revealing light to humanity.

> καὶ ἡ ζωὴ ἦν τὸ φῶς τῶν ἀνθρώπων (and the life was the light of humankind) (v 4).

Henceforth the metaphors used such as *logos*, *life* and *light* refer to Jesus without naming him. But the tragedy of rejection begins with a lack of understanding on the part of humanity,

> καὶ τὸ φῶς ἐν τῇ σκοτίᾳ φαίνει, καὶ ἡ σκοτία αὐτὸ οὐ κατέλαβεν. (but the light shines [historic present for shone] in the darkness and the darkness did not understand it) (v 5).

The word κατέλαβεν is translated 'understand' here instead of 'overcome' (as in I Thes 5:4) because in verse ten the writer says ὁ κόσμος αὐτὸν οὐκ ἔγνω, (the world did not recognize him), indicating cognition rather than conflict at this stage. The light and its function continue in the next few verses as an ordinary man, a prophet, was sent to bear witness to this light, but he was not the intended light. The real light having come into the world was intended to enlighten every human being, (v 9)

> Ἦν τὸ φῶς τὸ ἀληθινόν, ὃ φωτίζει πάντα ἄνθρωπον, ἐρχόμενον εἰς τὸν κόσμον, (There was the real light which enlightens every human being having come (when it comes) into the world).[8]

---

8. The phrase ἐρχόμενον εἰς τὸν κόσμον (having come into the world), could refer to every human being having come into the world, but the next verse refers back to the coming one and therefore it suggests that the participle ἐρχόμενον, (having come), refers to the light. God's purpose for the light coming into the world was to enlighten humanity.

But ironically Jesus was rejected by the world, verses 10 and 11. This is expressed by the analogies and metaphors used so far. The statement ἐν τῷ κόσμῳ ἦν grammatically refers to the light, 'it was in the world' as a metaphor for Jesus. The statement καὶ ὁ κόσμος δι' αὐτοῦ ἐγένετο (even though the world was made through him), has two possibilities of meaning. It is possible that John is thinking of Jesus metaphorically emerging from God like God's *logos* (speech) uttered to make the world that rejected him. It is also possible that he referred to Jesus in God by *synecdoche* when God made the world. The use of διά (through) supports the former interpretation. But Jesus as the agent of creation is difficult to envisage.

The mention of the world continues in the next clause, καὶ ὁ κόσμος αὐτὸν οὐκ ἔγνω, (and the world did not recognize him) refers directly to Jesus because of the use of the masculine pronoun αὐτόν (him). But Jesus' rejection is described in more surprising terms than this in v 11,

> εἰς τὰ ἴδια ἦλθεν καὶ οἱ ἴδιοι αὐτὸν οὐ παρέλαβον, (he came to his own [people], and his own [people] did not receive him).

This introduction of the rejection of God's Son becomes a recurring motif throughout the Gospel.

However, John continues with the idea of the revelation of God in Jesus in v 14 as a summarising statement, to say that the intention of God for revelation resulted in his human Son.

> Καὶ ὁ λόγος σὰρξ ἐγένετο καὶ ἐσκήνωσεν ἐν ἡμῖν, καὶ ἐθεασάμεθα τὴν δόξαν αὐτοῦ, δόξαν ὡς μονογενοῦς παρὰ πατρός, πλήρης χάριτος καὶ ἀληθείας. (And the *logos* became flesh and dwelt among us, and we beheld his glory, glory as of an only-begotten of the Father, full of grace and truth).

In a sense, God's *logos*, *intention*, could be perceived as God's seed giving rise to Jesus, the only-begotten of the Father. The glory that was beheld in the Son was described by Hebrews 1:3 as

> ὃς ὢν ἀπαύγασμα τῆς δόξης καὶ χαρακτὴρ τῆς ὑποστάσεως αὐτοῦ [τοῦ θεοῦ] (who was/is the brilliance shining from his [God's] glory and the character of his very being).

The word ἀπαύγασμα is constituted by ἀπό (from), and αὐγάζω, from αὐγή (daybreak or its radiance), to indicate an effulgence of light or glory from the Father shining in the Son.

John could not have understood the methodology proposed in this investigation. But he was not unaware that the father's seed was required to father an offspring, especially in a culture which believed that the father's seed was the only heritable element in one's conception. Further, it is very likely that John was aware of the events surrounding the conception of Jesus since Mary is said to have lived with John's family (Jn 19:26–27, assuming this beloved disciple was the author of the Gospel). It would be natural for Jesus' origin to have been shared with close friends. Besides, the 'birth narratives' had probably already been written and were circulating by the time John wrote. Therefore, John could detect the likeness of the only-begotten to his Father.

Unlike the opinion expressed by Dodd noted at the beginning of this chapter, it is likely that John did have knowledge of Jesus' conception and therefore of his origin and expressed it in verse thirteen of his prologue. The claims made in the previous few verses up to and including verse eleven fulfil the author's purpose to introduce the origin of his subject. But verse twelve advances the introduction to arrive at the means of salvation for believers through him. Thus,

> ὅσοι δὲ ἔλαβον αὐτόν, ἔδωκεν αὐτοῖς ἐξουσίαν τέκνα θεοῦ γενέσθαι, τοῖς πιστεύουσιν εἰς τὸ ὄνομα αὐτοῦ.
> (for as many as received him, to them he gave the right to become children of God, to those who believed in his name),
> [literally, in the name of him,]

The proximity of the pronoun αὐτοῦ (of him), at the end of verse twelve to the qualifying pronoun οἵ/ ὅς (who) at the beginning of verse thirteen suggests that the means of spiritual birth for believers described in verse thirteen, is faith in Jesus as the one who was born

> οὐκ ἐξ αἱμάτων οὐδὲ ἐκ θελήματος σαρκὸς οὐδὲ ἐκ θελήματος ἀνδρὸς ἀλλ' ἐκ θεοῦ [ἐγενήθη], [who was born] (not of bloods, nor of fleshly desire, nor of the will of a husband, but of God).

Therefore, verse thirteen seems to be speaking of God's literal fatherhood of Jesus. However, the best attested manuscripts have this pronoun in the plural οἵ (who) were born, referring to those who believe.

Argument for the singular pronoun and therefore a reference to Jesus' birth is proposed by Thomas F Torrance on several counts.[9] One is the use of the plural 'bloods' which suggests the involvement of two human beings in the birth of an offspring. Second, is the use of the 'flesh' which suggests human passion, and third, the use of a 'husband' instead of 'man', ἀνδρός instead of ἄνθρωπος, which suggests the will of the husband in a marriage wishing to produce offspring. Each is rejected by John as being the means of Jesus' birth.

Although Torrance concedes that the major manuscripts contain the plural pronoun, the Verna Old Latin (a manuscript significantly of Ephesian origin whence the Gospel was probably written) gives the singular. In addition, the main manuscripts are all from the fifth century.

> But there is considerable patristic evidence going back to the second and third centuries, Tertullian, Irenaeus, Justin Martyr, Epistola Apostolorum, and Hippolytus, and Clement of Alexandria—that is, all the available patristic evidence has John 1:13-14 in the singular at that date.[10]

Torrance refers to Tertullian (c155–220 CE) who claims that the Valentinians changed the singular to the plural because they did not like the idea of the virgin birth. All other texts were in the singular, and so the texts containing the singular are twice as old as the oldest of the main codices. Adolf von Harnack also claims that the singular is the true text which he believes is being increasingly followed by

---

9. Thomas F Torrance, *Incarnation: The Person and Life of Christ*, edited by RT Walker (Downers Grove, Illinois: IVP Academic, 2008), 89–91.
10. Although Torrance does not provide detailed references, some clearly confirm his claim, *The Ante-Nicene Fathers* Translation of the *Fathers down to AD 325*, edited by A Roberts and J Donaldson (Grand Rapids: Eerdmans, 1979), Volume III, Tertullian, 'On the Flesh of Christ', 537–538, 541 and fn 25; Volume I, Irenaeus, 'Against Heresies', 441 and 527 fn 1. The others refer to Jesus' parenthood, but not directly to the text in question.

scholars.[11] Barnabas Lindars opts for an analogy between the way Jesus was born and the way believers are also born spiritually.[12]

If Torrance's suggestion is correct, the singular reading in this verse provides reference to the virginal conception of Jesus in this Gospel. That is, that the *logos*, the Father's revelatory desire resulted in God's seed for the conception of Jesus. Though knowledge of procreation lacked the scientific details known today, it was certainly understood that it depended on the father. As mentioned earlier, Hebrews 7:4–10 has the offspring residing in the loins of its father, so to speak. Today one's origin being situated in one's parents is expressed by *synecdoche*, the figure of speech by which one's heredity is situated in one's parents and expressed as the residence of the whole offspring.

The use of *logos* rather than a father's seed is understandable. Apart from the likelihood that John was following the two means of God's revelation in prophecy and in a son, expressed in Hebrews 1:1, any mention of God's seed may have been misunderstood. Such a claim ran the risk of conjuring up in readers' minds the common belief in Hellenistic culture of gods having sexual intercourse with humans in the procreation of significant people.[13] Therefore, to avoid the thought of a similar methodology for the conception of Jesus, John maintains the use of *logos*.

Charles K Barrett believes that John found the birth narratives of Matthew and Luke misleading, suggesting that 'the notion of a virgin birth recalled pagan myths too clearly'.[14] However, it is possible that John uses Luke and Matthew's narratives to identify God as Jesus' literal Father. The *logos* idea seems to have made a lasting impression on John as summarised in verse fourteen above. At a time when John envisages the glorified and conquering Jesus riding a white horse in Revelation 19:11–16, he notes that his name is called ὁ λόγος τοῦ θεοῦ (the *logos* of God).[15]

---

11. Adolf von Harnack, *The Date of the Acts and the Synoptic Gospels*, translated by JR Wilkinson (London: Williams & Norgate, 1911), 148.
12. Barnabas Lindars, *The Gospel of John* (London: Oliphants, 1972), 91–93.
13. For example, the god Apollo with Amphictione for Plato's incarnation, the god Hermes with Penelope for the birth of Pan, and the goddess Aphrodite with Anchises for the birth of Aeneus.
14. Charles K Barrett, *The Gospel According to St John: An Introduction and Notes on the Greek Text* (London: SPCK, 1962), 125.
15. In some later manuscripts of I John 5:7-8 Jesus is again called 'the word', but this seems to be a later interpretive expansion as indicated in Aland, UBS *The Greek New Testament*, 819, fn 4.

For the sake of completeness, two more references to Jesus' alleged pre-existence are found in the Prologue. In verse fifteen, 'he who comes after me has surpassed me because he was before me', is often interpreted with a temporal meaning with the presupposition of Jesus' individual pre-existence before the Baptist. This meaning here is doubted by the context which is contrasting the status of each man, John and Jesus. It is more likely that the precedence of Jesus was being affirmed, very much like John 3:31 'the one who comes from above is above all'. Therefore, Jesus' pre-eminence is most likely meant in verse fifteen, rather than his pre-existence.

In addition, verse 18 is traditionally interpreted as saying that Jesus is 'God the Son' in a Trinity and was always an individual pre-existent in the bosom of the Father.

> θεὸν οὐδεὶς ἑώρακεν πώποτε· μονογενὴς θεὸς ὁ ὢν εἰς τὸν κόλπον τοῦ πατρὸς ἐκεῖνος ἐξηγήσατο (no one has ever seen God, the only-begotten God who is [was] in the bosom of [contained in] the father, he has explained him)

The word κόλπος, graphically translated 'bosom' and suggesting an embrace, could mean any 'space or indentation' within an object possessing the κόλπον including a geographical bay or gulf as in Acts 27:39. Therefore, the only-begotten being contained within the Father is an appropriate concept if the use of *synecdoche* is understood as being applied here. The designation μονογενὴς θεός, (the only begotten God) must refer to Jesus for the rest of the sentence to make sense. The reference to μονογενής, (the only-begotten), generally refers to Jesus and not to God.

The adjective μονογενής, (the only begotten) in the Bible always refers to an offspring and not to the uniqueness or γένος, (kind) of some other being like God.[16] Further, it is reasonable to translate μονογενής as the 'only-begotten' even though the word γεννάν, (to give birth), is not used, because a combination of μονο- and γεννάν is never found, either in the Bible or in biblical and non-biblical dictionaries.

---

16. In Luke 7:12; 9:38; Heb11:17 references are made to sons as the only offspring of a father or mother. In Luke 8:42 reference is to the only child, a daughter of a father, Jairus. In John 1:14; 3:16; 3:18; 1 Jn 4:9 all refer to Jesus as the only son of God.

Therefore, the usage of μονογενής to mean an only child is justified, and seems out of place in μονογενὴς θεός unless Jesus is called *God*. But to call Jesus 'God' would be unusual in the New Testament other than the instances discussed in chapter three to mean divine. In addition, rather than call Jesus 'God', John is more likely to have adopted Jesus' reported examples of insisting that he was the Son of God, and not in any sense thinking of trinitarian pre-existence. John AT Robinson is likely correct in regarding the original as μονογενὴς υἱός, (the only-begotten son) found in a number of ancient manuscripts instead of μονογενής θεός, (only-begotten God).[17] Robinson claims, 'I believe that θεός, God, may indeed be the best attested reading, and even go back to the autograph, but that it was a slip for υἱός, Son . . .'[18]

It is concluded that the prologue of John which is thought to provide proof that John considered Jesus to be pre-existent as an individual and being the agent of creation fails to show this. It is more likely that the pre-existence that John envisages here is that contained in God as the literal Father of Jesus, the source from which Jesus emerged.

Philippians 2:6–11

Another text which is interpreted in a way intended to prove Jesus' pre-existence as an individual is this famous text in Philippians. Here Paul is citing the greatest example of humility that has ever been demonstrated to encourage humility in the Philippian church. The example is that of Jesus' condescension from divine glory to humble humanity and finally to the cross. But Jesus' starting point in divinity is assumed to prove an individual existence as an equal being in a binitarian/trinitarian Godhead, because Jesus is said to have been in the form of God and equal with God. The presence of a second God equal to the first is avoided by a later patristic explanation of there being three equal persons (individuals) in the form of one God, and this supposedly avoids tri-theism.

---

17. The designation μονογενὴς θεός is found in Bodmer (p66) and in 75 among others, while some later manuscripts change it to μονογενὴς υἱός probably perceiving that a mistake was made. Irenaeus even combines it as μονογενὴς υἱὸς θεοῦ, Aland *et al*, UBS *The Greek New Testament*, 313.
18. Robinson, *Priority of John*, 372, 373.

The passage is found in a 'prison' letter written probably during or shortly after Paul's Caesarean imprisonment. If the historical situation was as indicated under 'The Testimony of Mary and Joseph' (chapter five), it is suggested that Paul's Christology may have undergone some clarification as a result of Luke's findings from Mary providing an understanding that God was Jesus' literal father. As God's offspring, Jesus, resided in the 'loins' of his father, so to speak, as in Hebrews 7:4–10, and therefore, was in the form of God and possessed qualitative equality with God. As noted earlier, the perception of offspring being in the father's loins is not entirely metaphorical, since there is a substantial (in substance) pattern which is inherited by the offspring even from generations past as in the case of Levi being in the loins of Abraham. Therefore, the idea in the Philippian statement is best described as making use of *synecdoche*. In the case of Jesus, the whole of Jesus is said to be within God, of the same form and having equality, when only part of Jesus, God's genetic contribution, was actually present in God's substance. To miss Paul's use of *synecdoche* here leads to unwarranted interactions between two deities, even though care is taken to avoid feelings of conflict between them.

Thus, ἐν μορφῇ θεοῦ ὑπάρχων, (existing in the form of God) is an understanding eminently suitable to a pre-existence as part of the spiritual substance of God, as described in methodology D2. Logically, one undifferentiated God-as-spirit is not partitioned. Therefore, any area of God being in the form of God and having equality with God could not conceivably be supposed an ἁρπαγμός, (a snatching) by any other area of God.

As a result of Mary's testimony via Luke, it is likely that Paul understood Jesus to have been part of God from whom he emerged as God's offspring, and therefore could be said to possess the form of God and qualitative equality with God in such pre-existence. The emergence of this part of God to give rise to the divine-human Jesus could be described as a humbling abandonment of a uniquely high status. This is described as an emptying himself of God-form and God-equality, and becoming mortal, even to the extent of dying a criminal's death on a cross. Yet Paul had encountered Jesus in blinding light in which he was exalted and glorified and he had no doubt as to his divinity. The atoning sacrifice having been completed, Jesus' exaltation to divine glory describes his deserved reward to receive the kind of worship appropriately offered to God.[19]

The Agency of Creation

The agency of creation of *all things* by Jesus is a further objection to a hereditary divinity since being the agent of creation, he would have pre-existed. Here, the wording πάντα and τὰ πάντα, (all things), mentioned in a number of texts is interpreted as referring to all things, the material universe, which were created by God and that they were created through the agency of the pre-existent Son. It is supposed that he was a member of an eternal Trinity and the agent of creation because of the association of the preposition διά (through) with 'all things'. In order to assess this interpretation, all the occurrences of the wording in the epistles and the Revelation are examined in order to identify the meaning of 'all things'.

Sixty-four references are identified, excluding those which use related forms of the word πάντα, (all things), and obviously meant something other than creation. Of the 64 instances in which the word πάντα, (all things), is used, twelve are possible references to creation. Prepositions such as ἐξ (from), and διά (by or through), suggest the origin of creation and an agent of creation respectively. Further, the association of words such as κτίσαντα and ἐποίησεν, (having built) or (created) and κατασκευάσας (constructed, built), in relation to τὰ πάντα (all things), certainly convey the meaning of the creation of the universe.

However, exegesis of these verses in their contexts provides alternative interpretations. The twelve texts are: Romans 11:36, 1 Corinthians 8:6, Ephesians 3:9, 4:10, Col 1:16-17, Hebrews 1:2, 1:3, Hebrews 2:8, 2:10, 3:4, Revelations 4:11, 21:5. Of these, five are in Paul, five in Hebrews, and two in Revelation. Seven of the total (Rom 11:36, Eph 3:9, Heb 2:8, Heb 2:10, Heb 3:2-4, Rev 4:21, 21:5) clearly refer to God rather than to Jesus as the creator or builder of all things. Two (Eph 4:10, Heb 2:8), speak of the glorified Jesus filling all things

---

19. Gordon D Fee, *Pauline Christology: An Exegetical-Theological study* (Peabody, Mass: Hendrickson Publishers, 2007), 373 claims that in quoting Isa 45:23, a statement by God about himself, and applying it to Jesus, Paul is in effect calling Jesus YHWH because the Septuagint translates the Hebrew word as Κύριος (Lord). This is unusual logic which is difficult to accept.

in the church and having all things subjected to him. This leaves four (1Cor 8:6, Col 1:16–17, Heb 1:2, Heb 1:3) for exegesis to assess the claim that Jesus was the agent of creation.

I Corinthians 8:6

This text is said to provide evidence for Jesus' pre-existence in the second of two clauses containing *all things* in the statement

> yet for us there is but one God, the Father, ἐξ οὗ τὰ πάντα (from whom all things [came]) καὶ ἡμεῖς εἰς αὐτόν (and for whom we live) and there is but one Lord, Jesus Christ, δι' οὗ τὰ πάντα (through whom all things [came], καὶ ἡμεῖς δι' αὐτοῦ (and through whom we live).

The historical context of this verse is a discussion about Christians eating food offered to idols, and Paul's concern is the salvation of the weaker brother (1Cor 8:7–13). A new or weaker Christian may see a mature or stronger one eating such food and may interpret this activity as honouring idols and consider that it is permissible for him or her to do the same. In this way the weaker person's faith may be diminished and even destroyed, a risk to be avoided at all costs.

The literary context of 8:6 is the contrast between pagans, who eat food offered to idols, and who worship 'gods many' and 'lords many' on the one hand, and on the other hand, Christians who believe in and worship 'one God, the Father', since we know that in reality 'there is no god but one' (v 4). The categories mentioned for pagans, 'gods and lords' are continued for Christians for whom they are limited to one of each, and each has his distinct function, providing the gift of salvation for Christians. In each case the gift, 'all things', is not elaborated, but the receiver's responsibility to the giver, from whom all things came, and the acknowledgement of benefit to the one through whom the gift came, provides the identification of 'all things'.

To the Father from whom the gift came, we are responsible for how we live. To the Lord Jesus Christ through whom it came, we acknowledge a debt for our privileged position, καὶ ἡμεῖς δι' αὐτου (through whom we live). The most obvious gift we have through him is redemption. Therefore, the obvious function for Jesus through whom 'all things came' is our salvation in this context, rather than our creation and this was initiated by the one God the Father, to whom we are responsible for the way we live.

Any attempt to make Jesus the agent of creation from the mention of 'all things' requires a manipulation of the text. Monotheism is acknowledged in the mention of our knowledge that 'there is no god but one'. However, the two functions mentioned require two individuals since God the Father did not die to redeem us, and could not have been the agent of redemption, even though he initiated it.

In order to overcome this difficulty, an attempt is made by Gordon Fee to include Jesus in the 'divine identity' and so in the Jewish *Shema*, asserting that there is one God, and by including Jesus in this, di-theism is supposedly avoided.[20] The inclusion of both into the Shema is said to be justified because they share a close relationship as father and son.[21]

Similarly, the idea of two deities sharing in one divine identity is proposed by Richard Bauckham in *Jesus and the God of Israel* where an attempt is made to describe a unity between Jesus and his Father by sharing the divine identity.[22] However, the idea is a puzzling concept as questioned by Dunn who claims that it is not a term which clarifies the relationship between God and Jesus because 'Jesus is not the God of Israel. He is not the Father. He is not Yahweh' and that the idea is similar to Modalism.[23]

The idea seems to have a verbal dependence rather than an ontological one. God is related to Israel in the revelation of his name YHWH, and to the creation in being its only creator (Isa 44:24) 'I alone stretched out the heavens'. As a result of these, God is the sovereign ruler of all things, and from the recognition of this identity, he alone is worshipped. The inclusion of Jesus in this divine identity by the writers of the New Testament is said to be shown by the fact that they and their congregations regarded Jesus as sovereign over all things, as creator of all, and because God has given him the divine name, according to Phil 2:9. As a result of this recognition, the early Christians worshipped Jesus.

---

20. Deuteronomy 6:4 claimed by Fee, *Pauline Christology*, 88.
21. Fee, *Pauline*, 90, 91.
22. Richard Bauckham, *Jesus and the God of Israel: God Crucified and Other Studies on the New Testament's Christology of Divine Identity* (Grand Rapids: Eerdmans, 2008).
23. James DG Dunn, *Did the First Christians worship Jesus? The New Testament Evidence* (London: SPCK, 2010), 142.

Apart from the philosophical arguments against the idea of including Jesus in the divine identity of God[24] the claims that Jesus created 'all things' have an alternative exegesis as pointed out in the prologue of John and will be discussed below. Therefore, his acclaim and worship was because of his redemption rather than from creating. As to God giving Jesus the divine name YHWH, the reasoning claims that the Jews replaced God's name with *Adonai* which is interpreted as 'Lord' as used in the Septuagint. The New Testament's favourite title for Jesus being 'Lord', it is therefore argued, that it is reasonable to trace his newly given name back through Adonai to YHWH. However, *Adonai* refers to 'Lord' and YHWH has the meaning 'the Being or he who is', hence the 'self-existent' or 'the eternal one'. Therefore, 'the name which is above every other name' of Phil 2:9 refers to an exaltation of one who is higher than any possible dignitary and this does not specify or include God.

Similar thinking is found in Ephesians 1:21. Here again Paul is speaking of Jesus' exaltation, καθίσας ἐν δεξιᾷ αὐτοῦ ... ὑπεράνω ... παντὸς ὀνόματος ὀνομαζομένου, (God ... having sat Jesus at his right above ... every name that is named). In neither case is a name specified, and by reference to 'name' the apostle was very likely expressing Jesus' lordship above every possible dignified entity. In any such discussions God is assumed to be unapproachably higher than anyone and is excluded from entities under anyone's lordship.

Therefore, in Philippians πᾶσα γλῶσσα ἐξομολογήσηται ὅτι κύριος Ἰησοῦς Χριστός, (every tongue will confess that Jesus Christ is Lord), refers to the overall lordship that Jesus is given by God with no other name being involved. Therefore, using this text to name Jesus YHWH is unconvincing, and the individualities of Jesus and of God are not blurred.

It is concluded that a more straight-forward reason for mentioning Jesus as Lord is the redemption he wrought for believers. Stated in different terms, Karl-Josef Kuschel agrees that 1Corinthians 8:6 has more to do with redemption than with cosmological creation.[25]

---

24. Dale Tuggy, *Theology Today*, 70/2 (2013): 128–143.
25. Karl-Joseph Kuschel, *Born Before All Time? The Dispute over Christ's Origin*, translated by J Bowden (London: SCM Press, 1992), 285–291. Kuschell enlists opinions for a meaning of redemption from J Murphy-O'Connor '1 Cor. 8:6: Cosmology or Soteriology', in *Review Biblique*, 85 (1998): 253–267, and a similar redemptive meaning rather than protological mediation of the first creation from Raymond Brown, *The Community of the Beloved Disciple* (New York: Paulist Press, 1979), 45, and J Dunn, *Christology*, 182.

Redemption is achieved through Jesus, through whom we have all the redemptive benefits that it brings.

Colossians 1:16–17

This is interpreted to mean that a pre-existent Jesus was the agent in whom or through whom all creation was built. The context is that God has rescued us and set us in the kingdom of his Son, in whom we have redemption, the forgiveness of sins. Verse fifteen describes him as the one who is the image of the invisible God, the firstborn or the pre-eminent above all creation, κτίσεως, (building). Verse sixteen further claims that he is first or pre-eminent because τὰ πάντα δι' αὐτοῦ καὶ εἰς αὐτὸν ἔκτισται (all things were built, and so created, through him and for him).

The claim that all the physical creation of God was created through Jesus as the agent of this creation has little support when the things built are nominated. The items are θρόνοι, κυριότητες, ἀρχαί, ἐξουσίαι, and again they are called τὰ πάντα (whether thrones, or powers [lordships], or rulers or authorities; all things were created by him and for him). This activity of creation or building (κτίσης) is used in the same sense as in 1 Peter 2:13. Building things other than physical is used by Peter speaking of ἀνθρωπίνη κτίσις (human authority) as in

> Ὑποτάγητε πάσῃ ἀνθρωπίνῃ κτίσῃ διὰ τὸν κύριον
> (submit yourselves to every human authority for the Lord).

The things *built* are nominated as

> εἴτε βασιλεῖ ὡς ὑπερέχοντι, εἴτε ἡγεμόσιν ὡς δι' αὐτοῦ πεμπομένοις εἰς ἐκδίκησιν κακοποιῶν... (whether to the king, as the supreme authority, or to governors, who are sent by him to those who do wrong...)

Therefore, the Colossian text refers to authority in the kingdom of God's Son, a kingdom in which various authorities are the result of his redeeming action, all [these] things were built though him and for him, rather than something that he built in pre-existence.

Hebrews 1:2

Hebrews 1:2 does not contain the wording 'all things', nevertheless the idea of the agency of Jesus may be implied from it. Here the subject is God and the agent is Jesus, but what was created is not the universe or the worlds as in the NIV and the NRSV, but the 'ages'. Thus, δι' οὗ καὶ ἐποίησεν τοὺς αἰῶνας (through whom [Jesus] he [God] made the ages).[26] The ages in the mind of a Hebrew and thence of a Christian would most naturally refer to the present age and the age to come. The coming of Jesus marks the end event of one age and the ushering in of the second, even though the second does not properly begin until Jesus' return. Thus through him God has designated the ages and many of the benefits of the age to come have begun to be experienced in this present age because of Jesus' first coming.

The fact that in Hebrews 11:3 κατηρτίσθαι τοὺς αἰῶνας ῥήματι θεοῦ refers to the (creation of the universe by the word of God) does not change the meaning that ages has in Hebrews 1:2. The context of 11:3 is the activity by which the invisible became visible, whereas in 1:2 the context is the change in the means of God's revelation in time, and therefore *age* seems more appropriate as the time of the coming of the Son inaugurating a new age.[27]

Hebrews 1:3

Hebrews 1:3 does contain a mention of 'all things' describing the Son as

> ὅς ὢν ἀπαύγασμα τῆς δόξης καὶ χαρακτὴρ τῆς ὑποστάσεως αὐτοῦ (being the radiance of God's glory and the exact representation of his [God's] hypostasis)

as interpreted under the Prologue. But the text which suggests creativity or power over the physical creation is the next statement,

---

26. The word αἰών, means a period of existence, a definite space of time. A temporal understanding is the usual meaning of the word rather than creation (Liddell and Scott's Greek-English Lexicon does not mention a creational meaning). But HK Moulton, *Analytical Greek Lexicon* Revised 1978, states that 'by an Aramaism οἱ αἰῶνες can have the meaning of the material universe'. Therefore, the meaning depends on the context.
27. The distinction between 'this age' and 'the age to come' is expounded by George L Ladd, *The Gospel of the Kingdom* (Grand Rapids: Eerdmans, 1959), 28, 35, 38, 42.

φέρων τε τὰ πάντα τῷ ῥήματι τῆς δυνάμεως αὐτοῦ.
(sustaining all things by his powerful word)

When the words are taken at face value in English, the one who is the exact likeness of God sustains, and has sustained, the universe from its creation.

But the context is about God's new revelation in a Son who achieved redemption. The words φέρων and ῥήματι have semantic ranges greater than the two meanings given in the NRSV and NIV, of 'sustaining' and 'powerful word'. For example, φέρων has meanings of carrying, enduring, bringing, establishing, sustaining, and even suffering as in ὑποφέρων. The word ῥῆμα may mean a saying, a will, a thing, a matter, an event, or a happening. Further, there is a variant in verse three [28]

τῷ ῥήματι τῆς δυνάμεως, δι' ἑαυτοῦ καθαρισμόν τῶν ἁμαρτιῶν ποιησάμενος, (by the will of the power, through himself having made a cleansing of sins),

instead of τῷ ῥήματι τῆς δυνάμεως αὐτοῦ (the word of his power). This indicates a closely connected progression in the three clauses which describe the achievements of the Son. The progression is:

(1) φέρων τε τὰ πάντα τῷ ῥήματι τῆς δυνάμεως,
(enduring all things according to the will of God)

'Power' is a synonym for God as in Mark 14:62 and parallels in Matthew 26:64 and Luke 22:69.

(2) δι' ἑαυτοῦ καθαρισμὸν τῶν ἁμαρτιῶν ποιησάμενος
(through himself having made purification for sins)

(3) ἐκάθησεν ἐν δεξιᾷ τῆς μεγαλοσύνης ἐν ὑψηλοῖς (he sat down on the right of the majesty on high).

No such logical progression is evident in the commonly accepted phraseology in which there is no connection between making purification for sins and sustaining the universe. Thus it may be understood that the first of the three clauses φέρων τε τὰ πάντα

---

28. Barbara Aland, *et al* editors of fourth edition, UBS *The Greek New Testament*, 741

(enduring all things), is redemptive rather than cosmological, and the passage does not necessarily refer to the Son's power in creating and sustaining the universe, but to the redemption which he wrought by his obedient suffering. As a result of this achievement he is highly exalted.

It may be seen from these twelve texts incorporating fourteen mentions of 'all things' that only the two in Revelation clearly refer to the physical creation, and this is not a situation involving the pre-existent Jesus, but refers to the consummation of God's salvation. In the exegesis of the remaining texts it has been shown that the mention of 'all things' does not automatically refer to the physical creation, but to redemption and to the authority that Jesus deserves as a result of it. The adoption of a cosmological meaning in order to make Jesus the agent of creation and therefore pre-existent is not convincing. Therefore, it may be said that Jesus is the agent of redemption, but not the agent of creation. As has been mentioned already, the part of the substance of God which contributed to Jesus' ontology was originally part of the creator God, and this might justly designate Jesus as creator God by *synecdoche*, but not simply as the agent of such creation.

Chapter Seven
Implication for the Doctrine of the Trinity

If the methodology for a genetically inherited divinity of Jesus is correct, it becomes foundational for theological statements of various doctrines, particularly the doctrine of the Trinity. In an endeavour to clarify its implications for this doctrine a borrowed statement from James Dunn seems appropriate.

> we must attempt the exceedingly difficult task of shutting out the voices of the Fathers, Councils and dogmaticians down the centuries, in case they drown the earlier voices, in case the earlier voices [of New Testament writers] . . . intended their words to speak with different force to their hearers.[1]

Therefore, in the following discussion on the Trinity the long history of trinitarian claims of patristic theologians and later dogmaticians will not be detailed. A large number of ideas have been expressed on this subject, probably due to the uncertainty of what is written about it in the scriptures. In modern times a useful summary is presented by Robert Letham.[2]

The doctrine of the Trinity faces explanatory difficulties in trying to match biblical statements concerning monotheism with other statements which lead to a belief in the existence of three eternal divine individuals, the Father, Son and Holy Spirit. The situation is proclaimed in a catch-phrase which has come down through history as μία οὐσία, τρεῖς ὑποστάσεις (one substance [in] three

---

1. Dunn, *Christology*, 13, the advice is applicable here as well, although Dunn is speaking of Christology in general.
2. Robert Letham, *The Holy Trinity, In Scripture, History, Theology, and Worship* (New Jersey, USA: P&R Publishing, 2004)

hypostaseis [individuals, persons]).³ It is repeated frequently as 'God in three persons' and 'God, the three in one'. The mental gymnastics involved in trying to make sense of this give rise to theological comments which are sometimes contradictory to one another.

Endeavours to explain God's threeness and oneness either begin with God's oneness and try to discover ways in which one God could simultaneously be three persons (the so-called Latin Trinitarianism), or begin with three persons and try to discover how three persons could simultaneously be one God (the so-called Social Trinitarianism).⁴ However, though assuming monotheism, the New Testament seems to refer to three divine individuals without attempting to unite them into a trinity. Therefore, it may be argued that

> the New Testament contains no doctrine of the Trinity . . . . The New Testament writers and the congregations for whom they wrote understood themselves as monotheists . . . The Shema, with its emphatic statement of God's exclusiveness . . . is something to be taken for granted . . . throughout the Bible.⁵

The obvious incongruity in having one God in three persons was not a consideration of biblical writers to explain.

Monotheism as revealed to the Hebrew people in the well-known *Shema* (Deut 6:4 'Hear Israel, The Lord our God, the Lord is one') logically implies that any further deities must have arisen without being created from the substance of God the Father. The concept is supported historically by the birth of Jesus, as God's Son, and by the giving of the Spirit at Pentecost.

But confusion arises from the interpretation of texts which suggest Jesus' pre-existence as discussed in chapter six and by the use of the word 'spirit' used in the Bible before Pentecost. The distinction between the Pentecostal Spirit and spirit, Spirit Holy, and Holy Spirit pre-Pentecost to refer to God-as-spirit is a worthwhile observation. It has been so interpreted by James Dunn in *Christology in the Making*

---

3. The history of the formula has been traced by Joseph T Lienhard, '*Ousia* and *Hypostasis: The Cappadocian Settlement and the Theology of "one Hypostasis,"*' in *The Trinity: An Interdisciplinary Symposium on the Trinity* edited by Stephen T Davis, Daniel Kendall, Gerald O'Collins (Oxford: Oxford University Press, 1999), 99–121.
4. Brian Leftow, 'Anti-Social Trinitarianism', *Trinity*, 203
5. Donald H Juel, 'The Trinity and the New Testament', *Theology Today*, 54 (1997): 313.

and by Geoffrey WH Lampe in *God as Spirit: The Bampton Lectures* and referred to in chapter five, footnote 16. Therefore, the origin of the Son and the Spirit from the Father in time seems possible and according to this investigation it is supported by substantial evidence.

Two categories of trinitarian existence in God may be deduced, a derived and an underived Trinity. An underived Trinity is the traditionally developed and most popular idea of one God existing as three individuals, Father, Son and Holy Spirit and yet somehow united. Their individuality and unity is qualified with words which seek to differentiate this from tri-theism. The second category, a derived Trinity, is implied by the concept of monotheism. As suggested above, this implies that any further deities in addition to the one God would have arisen in some way from the one God. To be divine, any derived deities would not have been created, but would have emerged in some way from the substance of God. As originator, this deity could be called Father. However, the two derived divinities could have emerged in pre-history or in history.

It is difficult to imagine the emergence of two further divinities in eternity and to contemplate the purpose for such emergence. A purpose for the eternal emergence of the Son and of the Spirit is suggested by Richard Swinburne in *Was Jesus God?* The reason given is that on the basis of the need of loving persons to love, God who is a perfectly loving person, needed someone equal to himself to love and brought into existence the Son. The two cooperated in sharing love with a third, the Holy Spirit, whom they brought into existence for the same purpose, to have a third person to love forming a Trinity of divine persons.[6]

The emergence of the Son from the Father in history has been discussed at length in this investigation. The emergence of the Spirit historically is explained by the apostle Peter giving a reason for the events of Pentecost to the amazed crowd in Acts 2:17 quoting from Joel 2:28. Thus, ἐκχεῶ ἀπὸ τοῦ πνεύματός μου ἐπὶ πᾶσαν σάρκα (I will pour out (or spill) from my spirit upon all flesh), and the phraseology is repeated in verse eighteen. This suggests that

---

6. Richard Swinburne, *Was Jesus God?* (Oxford: Oxford University Press, 2008), 28–30. Mutual love in the Trinity in eternity is emphasised by Richard of St. Victor in Book Three, 'Of the Trinity' in *Richard of St. Victor: The Twelve Patriarchs, The Mystical Ark, Book Three of the Trinity*, translated by Grover A Zinn (London: SPCK, 1979), 373–397.

God poured out some of his spiritual substance as the Holy Spirit on the day of Pentecost. The phrase 'from my spirit' is found in the Septuagint version of Joel and is repeated in Acts in the Greek ancient and modern versions, but it is omitted in the English versions. It is of interest that a parenthetical statement in John 7:39 affirms οὔπω γὰρ ἦν πνεῦμα, ὅτι᾽ Ἰησοῦς οὐδέπω ἐδοξάσθη (for the Spirit was not yet, because Jesus had not yet been glorified). Some later manuscripts add δεδομένον (given), perhaps in order to offset the possible perception that Pentecost was the beginning of the Holy Spirit as an individual *hypostasis*.

In this spillage of God's substance God-as-spirit who is the source and the emergent Spirit are of the same and unchanged spiritual substance. It may even be possible to believe that God-as-spirit and the Holy Spirit are not two *hypostaseis* but one, so that God-as-spirit came upon the disciples at Pentecost. The evidence for the Holy Spirit being a new emergent individual depends largely on the way in which Jesus spoke about it. Statements such as Jn 16:7

> ἐὰν γὰρ μὴ ἀπέλθω, ὁ παράκλητος οὐκ ἐλεύσεται (for if I do not go away, the Paraclete will not come), ἐὰν δὲ πορευθῶ, πέμψω αὐτὸν πρὸς ὑμᾶς (but if I go, I will send him to you)

These words are less likely to be referring to God-as-spirit and more likely to refer to another *hypostasis*, the Holy Spirit.

Even though the statements could be seen to be referring to an already existent individual in heaven ready to be sent by Jesus on his return there, previous statements by Jesus in John 14:16, 26 affirm that it is the Father who will send the Paraclete.

> κἀγὼ ἐρωτήσω τὸν πατέρα καὶ ἄλλον παράκλητον δώσει ὑμῖν, (and I will ask the father and he will send another *paraclete* to you) ὁ δὲ παράκλητος, τὸ πνεῦμα τὸ ἅγιον, ὃ πέμψει ὁ πατὴρ ἐν τῷ ὀνόματί μου, ἐκεῖνος διδάξει πάντα καὶ ὑπομνήσει ὑμᾶς πάντα ἃ εἶπον ὑμῖν [ἐγώ] (and the *paraclete*, the Holy Spirit, whom the Father will send in my name, he will teach you and remind you all that I have told you)

Therefore, Jesus' statement in John 16:7 that he will send the *Paraclete* may be referring to the sequence of events in the redemptive process which depended on himself and his work, including his resurrection and ascension. In that case, it is reasonable to consider the Pentecostal Spirit as an individual very similar to God-as-spirit, emerging from God and performing a particular function in the church and in individual believers.

It is virtually impossible to contemplate these ideas without remembering that similar statements were voiced by the Church Fathers. The Cappadocian theologians, who consolidated the idea of the Trinity in the fourth century, in some of their statements could be interpreted as having in mind such origins for the Son and the Spirit. Basil distinguishes the three members of the Trinity as the Father who is characterised by πατρότης (paternity), the Son by υἱότης, (sonship), and the Spirit by ἁγιοστικῆ δύναμις (sanctifying power) or ἁγιασμός (sanctification).[7] Gregory of Nazianzus characterises them similarly by ἀγεννησία (ingeneratedness, non-birth), for the Father, γέννησις (birth) for the Son and ἐκπόρευσις (procession out of) for the Spirit.[8]

However, in other statements there is a lingering perception that the divine persons were individuals in eternity and that any emergence took place before the derived deities appeared in history. Their appearances are described as their τρόποι ὑπάρξεως (modes of existing) or even (of becoming).[9] It is thought by some that somehow the three may have been individuals in eternity and either that there was no emergence from the Father or that the derivation of the Son and the Spirit from the Father somehow occurred in eternity.

In the eighth century John of Damascus writes with some ambiguity in Περί τῆς Ἁγίας Τριάδος, *About the Holy Trinity*.[10] In the first statement (below) the three divinities are described as being ὁμοούσιοι καὶ ἄκτισται ὑπάρχουσι (they exist of the same substance and are uncreated). He does not clearly differentiate the epoch of their existence, but he is probably thinking of pre-history.

---

7. John ND Kelly *Early Christian Doctrines*, revised edition, (Massachusetts: Prince Press, Harper Collins, 2004), 265.
8. John ND Kelly *Early Christian Doctrines*, 265.
9. John ND Kelly *Early Christian Doctrines*, 266
10. John of Damascus, *De fide orthodoxa* (*An Exact Exposition of the Orthodox Faith*) Ἰωάννου Δαμασκοῦ, Ἔκδοσις Ἀκριβὴς τῆς Ὀρθοδόξου Πίστεως, Μετάφραση Νίκου Ματσούκα, Ἐκδόσεις ΙΙ. (Πουρναρά, Θεσσαλονίκη, 1985), 56.

> Κατὰ μὲν οὖν τὸ πρῶτον σημαινόμενον κοινωνοῦσιν αἱ τρεῖς τῆς ἁγίας θεότητος ὑπέρθεοι ὑποστάσεις ὁμοούσιοι γὰρ καὶ ἄκτισται ὑπάρχουσι
> (According to the first principle the three most divine hypostaseis (or individuals or persons) of the holy divinity are in fellowship for they exist of the same substance and are uncreated)

But in the descriptions of each divinity the only one who is not derived from any other individual is the Father. The other two are derived from the Father by two different means.

> Κατὰ δὲ τὸ δεύτερον σημαιόμενον οὐδαμῶς μόνος γὰρ ὁ Πατὴρ ἀγέννητος. οὐ γὰρ ἐξ ἑτέρας ἐστιν αὐτῷ ὑποστάσεως τὸ εἶναι
> (According to the second principle and in no other way the Father alone is unborn. There is no other hypostasis (or individuality) from which he was derived).

> καὶ μόνος ὁ Υἱὸς γεννητός ἐκ τῆς τοῦ Πατρὸς γὰρ οὐσίας ἀνάρχως καὶ ἀχρόνως
> (and the Son alone is begotten [born] of the Father's substance without a beginning and timelessly)

> καὶ μόνον τὸ Πνεῦμα τὸ Ἅγιον ἐκπορευτὸν ἐκ τῆς οὐσίας τοῦ Πατρός, οὐ γεννόμενον ἀλλ' ἐκπορευόμενον
> (and the Holy Spirit alone having proceeded from the substance of the Father, not begotten [not born], but having proceeded).

Thus the Father is described as ἀγέννητος (unborn), the Son as γεννητός (born), and the Spirit as ἐκπορευτόν (having proceeded) and not by birth. The derived divinities are said to have emerged from the Father's οὐσία (substance). Yet the Son's method of birthing is described by two adverbs as being ἀνάρχως (without beginning), and ἀχρόνως (timelessly). The author seems to be wavering between events occurring in time and in eternity.

Whatever may be the reality, the derivation of the Son and the Spirit from the Father seems to be a basic understanding and is consistent with the idea of monotheism. The idea that there were three Gods in eternity contradicts monotheism however their unification may be imagined. It also contradicts historical revelation in the birth of Jesus and the coming of the Spirit, and relies on perceptions of the meaning of statements affirming Jesus' pre-existence as described earlier. It may be concluded that the methodology of the coming of Jesus into the world is a key perception for this doctrine. Either a pre-existent divinity became incarnate into Mary's womb, or part of God became incarnate in Mary's ovum cell. The latter seems to be a more reasonable methodology.

The word 'trinity' suggests some kind of ontological unity between three individuals who would otherwise be perceived to be a tri-theistic company. The ancient theologians were aware of the problem as a contradiction to monotheism and commandeered the concept of περιχώρησις, *perichoresis*, often translated as permeation or interpenetration of each individual into the being or substance of the others.

The word περιχώρησις which is composed by περί and χωρέω has a long history which has been traced by Slobodan Stamatovic in 'The Meaning of Perichoresis' in *Open Theology 2* (2016).[11] He shows convincingly that the meaning which the word had in Classical Greek and given in Classical Greek dictionaries has changed from 'moving around in an area' to the meaning which it conveyed in Koine Greek. It is used in patristic writings with the meaning of 'having' or 'making room for' or 'containing' and even 'to permeate' and 'interpenetrate'. With this understanding the basic part χωρέω (I contain), (I have room for), is found in several instances in the New Testament (Mat 15:17, 19:11, Mk 2:2, Jn 2:6, 8:37, 21:25, 2Cor 7:2, 2Pet 3:9). For example, in Jn 8:37 Jesus says to the Jews οἶδα ὅτι σπέρμα' Ἀβραάμ ἐστε ἀλλὰ ζητεῖτε μὲ ἀποκτεῖναι, ὅτι ὁ λόγος ὁ ἐμὸς οὐ χωρεῖ ἐν ὑμῖν (I know that you are Abraham's seed but you are seeking to kill me, because my word has not penetrated you or permeated your heart).

The prefix περί may have retained its meaning (around) to refer to the *perichoresis*, (interpenetration) operating around the three divine entities.[12] The combined word περιχώρησις *perichoresis* is thought to have been used first by Gregory of Nazianzus in the fourth century to affirm the unity of the two natures of Christ, the divine and the human. He says,

---

11. Slobodan Stamativic, <https://www.academia.edu/25424100/> The Meaning of Perichoresis Open Theology 2 20 16.
12. Unfortunately, some have confused χωρέω, (contain), with χορεύω, (I dance), and have imagined a dancing Trinity.

κριναμένων ὥσπερ τῶν φύσεων, οὕτω δὴ καὶ τῶν κλήσεων καὶ περιχωρουσῶν εἰς ἀλλήλας τῷ λόγῳ τῆς συμφυΐας
(being judged that just like the natures, so it is with the titles, they are interwoven into one another by reason of their cohesion).[13]

In his use of the word *perichoresis* Gregory is obviously commenting on the unity of natures and not on trinitarian unity. John of Damascus was aware of Gregory's writing and refers to it in his *De fide orthodoxa*, Ἔκδοσις ἀκριβὴς τῆς ὀρθοδόξου πίστεως. He wants to express the divinity of the whole of Christ. He understands Gregory to be saying that Christ's nature did not change or switch from one to another or become of another kind or copied to become divine.[14]

ὥς φησιν ὁ θεολόγος Γρηγόριος ... Ταῦτα γὰρ οὐ κατὰ μεταβολὴν φύσεως, ἀλλὰ κατὰ τὴν οἰκονομικὴν ἕνωσιν, τὴν καθ' ὑπόστασιν λέγω, καθ' ἥν ἀδιασπάστως τῷ Θεῷ Λόγῳ ἥνωνται, καὶ τὴν ἐν ἀλλήλαις τῶν φύσεων περιχώρησιν
(As the theologian Gregory says ... for these happened not by a change in his nature, but by the economic unity by which I say his hypostasis was not torn asunder, being united in the Divine Word, and the natures permeated each other).

Elsewhere, unlike Gregory who used *perichoresis* to describe the unity of the natures of Christ, John uses the same word to describe the unity experienced by the three divine individuals or persons. He says[15]

ἐνοῦνται γὰρ, ὡς ἔφημεν, οὐχ ὥστε συγχεῖσθαι, ἀλλ' ὥστε ἔχεσθαι ἀλλήλων· καὶ τὴν ἐν ἀλλήλαις περιχώρησιν ἔχουσιν δίχα πάσης συναλοιφῆς καὶ συμφύρσεως
(for they are united, as we have said, not in the sense of mixing (συγχεῖσθαι) but in the sense of possessing each other by reason of mutual perichoresis or permeation without any blending and mingling).

---

13. Gregory of Nazianzus in J Migne, *Patrologia Graeca* Epistle 101, columns 181, 182.
14. John of Damascus, Ἔκδοσις, 294.
15. John of Damascus, Ἔκδοσις, 66

Thus, without a sense of dissolution of the derived individuals into the substance of the originator, the three divine individuals are so united ontologically by a mutual interpenetration or permeation that they may be perceived to be one God. But this does not specify whether the *perichoresis* was operative in pre-history or in history in the economy of salvation. This investigation depicting a methodology for the coming into the world of God's Son in time and for the contingency of human salvation obviously favours a historically derived Trinity. In the case of such Trinity, a reunification of the two emergent divinities may be understood, so that the three now exist as three individuals with the perfect unity as well as individuality conveyed by *perichoresis*.

A reunification is hinted at by Jesus in Jn 14:28 towards the end of his earthly life when he expressed a desire to return to the place from which he came, to God πορεύομαι πρὸς τὸν πατέρα, (I go to the Father), and with greater explanation in Jn16:28,

> ἐξῆλθον παρὰ τοῦ πατρὸς καὶ ἐλήλυθα εἰς τὸν κόσμον. Πάλιν ἀφίημι τὸν κόσμον καὶ πορεύομαι πρὸς τὸν πατέρα (I came forth or emerged from the Father and have come into the world; again, I leave the world and go to the Father).

It is possible to understand his destination to be a spiritual place or realm or condition, but his destination may even be referring to God's spiritual substance whence he originated genetically. If God's presence or condition may be designated *glory* which Jesus experienced in his pre-existence by *synecdoche* in the substance of the Father, then Jesus' request in Jn 17:5 expresses a longing to return. His request,

> καὶ νῦν δόξασόν με σύ, πάτερ, παρὰ σεαυτῷ τῇ δόξῃ ᾗ εἶχον πρὸ τοῦ τὸν κόσμον εἶναι παρὰ σοί, (and now glorify me, Father, with the glory I had with you before the world was made),

may be referring to this destination. Therefore his expressed desire to return to this glory may be seen as a desire for reunion into God's substance, constituting an ontological union and therefore a *binity*. As mentioned, it is not suggested that the glorified Jesus was absorbed and dissolved into the substance of God, since he is spoken of many times as a continuing individual after this glorification. As such an individual, having returned to be within the substance of God, he appeared to Paul on the way to Damascus where a light from the sky shone around him with a voice claiming to be Jesus (Acts 9:3).

In the case of the Holy Spirit a reunion or continuing union seems relatively easy to understand. God-as-spirit who was the source and the emergent Spirit are of the same and unchanged spiritual substance. The ontological connection between the two divine spirits, God-as-spirit and the Holy Spirit, both being omnipresent and dwelling within each other seems feasible. In that case a further *binity* could be understood, and with Jesus present, it constitutes the ontological Trinity. In this situation it is suggested that the Son and the Spirit are also united by *perichoresis*.

The greatness of God does not give any indication of size. But from human experience the seed of an entity might suggest that that which emerged would be a relatively small part of the originating entity. If it is the case that a relatively small part of the substance of a very great God emerged to miraculously materialize within an ovum cell contributed by Mary, it is likely that the glorified Son is also a relatively small part of God. This view is not intended to belittle Jesus who is sufficient for all that humanity requires for salvation or to fulfil any plans of God to place all things under his lordship (Eph 1:10), but to face the reality of the greatness of God. A similar view may apply to the Holy Spirit which, though perhaps emerging as a relatively small part of the spirit that is God, it is all that humanity will ever require to function as the people of God. If this is the reality, then two great *hypostaseis* with separate spiritual substances are contained within the spiritual substance of a greater *hypostasis* forming an ontological Trinity.

The individuals described as sharing an ontological unity share in the attributes, purposes, actions, decisions and authority of one God and are together omnipresent, and together receive worship. What is uttered by worshippers specifying one hypostasis is not hidden from the other two, nor could it generate envy since they are united not only in agreement, but ontologically as well. The question posed in chapter 3 under the worship of Jesus whether Jesus should be worshipped in the same way as the Father loses its uncertainty when their present unity is in view.

The concept of the assessment of greatness leads naturally into the idea of subordination of the two emergent *hypostaseis* to the originator. This is a perennial point of contention among theologians, but it seems needless, since apart from their derivation, there seems to be no need for any form of instruction or command from one to another.

It is concluded that the methodology proposed for a genetically inherited divinity for Jesus does have implications for the doctrine of the Trinity. Therefore, the Christian is left to consider the evidence between two possibilities for the state of the existence of God in eternity and now. Either there were three individual deities called Father, Son and Holy Spirit, or there was one deity who gave rise to the other two by two different means. As history is revealed, these events occurred in time for the purpose of human redemption. The gracious generosity of God towards humanity is thus revealed and generates human amazement, gratitude and worship.

Conclusion

The existence of God who made the universe and the revelation from him to human beings in the biblical writings are two proposals which have been verified with evidence by others. The ancient writings provide evidence concerning Jesus of Nazareth who was sent by God into the world over two thousand years ago to redeem lost humanity. Because of his resurrection from death, he still lives today and may be called upon for salvation. God's demand upon human beings is to trust the living redeemer for individual forgiveness. In order to believe in him, human beings require evidence for his capability to fulfil the required redemption. Therefore, his nature or ontology is the starting point for people's consideration of him as one who is able to reconcile them with God. Evidence for his ontology has been the main concern of this writing.

Jesus' work of redemption required his death as an offering to God for human sin. For this to happen he needed to be human. The evidence for his real humanity is adequately provided, not only by his appearance and way of life, but also by the way physiological processes were operating in his body to bring about his death on the cross. For his death to be efficacious for the sins of humanity he was required to be a sinless offering to God. As no mere human being could fulfil this requirement, he was also provided with a divine nature. The major evidence for his divinity is his resurrection from death. This also indicated God's approval and acceptance of his sacrifice for human sin. Human persons considering this sacrifice as their offering to God for their sinfulness receive forgiveness and are reconciled to God.

The ultimate indicator for the human and divine ontology of Jesus has been shown to be the methodology of his conception from human and divine parents. This was a supernatural event in which some of the spiritual substance of God materialized inside an ovum cell released from one of Mary's ovaries after ovulation. This is far removed from a sexual act or an insemination as no semen or sperm were involved. Materialization of God's spiritual substance may be called an incarnation, the conversion of spiritual substance into 'flesh'. The methodology complies with the concept of monotheism, belief in the existence of one and only God.

Biblical support for the methodology was found in texts which indicated God's literal fatherhood of Jesus. Some objections to the methodology based on texts which suggested the incarnation of a pre-historic individual deity who was also the agent of God for the creation have been shown to have alternative interpretations. Therefore, the objections do not annul the methodology. The Holy Spirit has also been shown to have emerged from God's spiritual substance but by a different method which did not require any change in spiritual form.

Today, a trinity of divine individuals is proposed, consisting of the two derived divine beings which are united in the substance of the originator, God the Father. In this way they are united in their substances while maintaining their individualities. In such existence they are also united in their omnipresence and their purposes and therefore they all receive worship and respond to the prayers of their believing people.

Lightning Source UK Ltd.
Milton Keynes UK
UKHW012111030123
414771UK00005B/834